MARITIME HERITAGE

White's of Cowes

'White's-built, well-built!'

A carnival occasion, the launch of the destroyer *Fury* **on 10 September 1934. The crowd of onlookers clearly includes the wives and children of yard workers.** *White's Archives, Cowes Maritime Museum*

Aerial view of the shipyard on 9 June 1934. The fitting-out quays at West Cowes, on the far side, are empty, but in a well-advanced state of construction on the slipways at East Cowes are the destroyers *Forester*, on the right, and *Fury*. In the river at the right is the Cowes Floating Bridge Number 2, another product of the White's shipyard, delivered in 1925. *Aerofilms*

Maritime Heritage

White's of Cowes

'White's-built, well-built!'

David L. Williams

Silver Link Publishing Ltd

© David L. Williams 1993

First published in August 1993

British Library Cataloguing in Publication Data
A catalogue record for this book is available from the British Library

ISBN 0 85794 011 3

Silver Link Publishing Ltd
Unit 5
Home Farm Close
Church Street
Wadenhoe
Peterborough PE8 5TE
Tel/fax (08015) 4-4-0

Printed and bound in Great Britain

Title page **HMS *Faulknor* completing at West Cowes beneath the famous hammer-head crane; she had been launched as the Chilean destroyer leader *Almirante Simpson* on 26 February 1914. At the Battle of Jutland the *Faulknor* led the attack on the German 2nd Battle Squadron.** *White's Archives, Cowes Maritime Museum*

ACKNOWLEDGEMENTS

When I was invited by the Isle of Wight branch of the World Ship Society to investigate the possibility of getting Ray Sprake's research material on the White's shipyard published in some form, I felt most honoured and was pleased to do whatever I could. Thanks to Silver Link's interest in the topic, I have been able to produce a completely new manuscript based on Ray's material, although because of publishing schedules this had to be achieved in near record time, an aspect of the project which gave me more than the usual problems. Fortunately, I had the benefit of an extra boost to my fortitude, helping me to weather those stresses and strains that arose, and that was the ever-present knowledge of the pleasure it would have given Ray Sprake to see a new book on White's in print, as the realisation of his ambitions.

In fact, it has been a pleasurable and fascinating experience to write about a subject of local interest, immersing myself in history that has happened right on my 'doorstep'. Also, through my own long friendship with Ray Sprake, the creation of this book has been very much a 'labour of love' during which I have derived great satisfaction and pleasure from the generous assistance and contributions of material from numerous individuals, organisations and companies, many quite evidently made as tokens of regard for Ray himself.

Accordingly, I would like here to record my appreciation for that help, in whatever form it took, all of which enabled me to achieve the successful completion of this book. While these thanks are extended to all concerned, I would like, in addition, to make particular mention of the following people:

Mrs Katherine Harrison at the Cowes Maritime Museum, whose intimate knowledge of White's history and of the contents of that part of the Company archives now housed in the Museum permitted the unearthing of many useful snippets of information and additional items of material worthy of inclusion.

David Burdett and Paul Ebbatson of East Cowes Heritage, a sub-group of the Isle of Wight Society, for their assistance with photographs.

Mervyn Pearson, who was a fitter in the J. Samuel White shipyard from 1950 to 1955, who deserves my very special thanks for the cover picture, specially painted for the book, as well as for the entertainment of his many stories and anecdotes from his time in the yard.

Ron Trowell, who started work in 1937 in the Engine Drawing Office at the J. Samuel White shipyard, later becoming the Company's Publicity Manager, a position he held up to 1965. Ron was responsible for taking all the official Company photographs from the early 1950s until the yard's closure, all of which material he very generously placed at my disposal.

Nick Henry for assisting with printing copy negatives of early White's paintings as well as a number of my own original negatives.

Mr C. D. Webster and the staff at the Isle of Wight Records Office for their assistance with research of old maps of the East and West Cowes waterfronts.

Richard de Kerbrech, my good friend and co-author on previous books, who with his usual enthusiasm sought out many pictures and other useful material for the book.

Jochen Krüsmann, who helped to clarify numerous discrepancies relating to the vessels built for Turkish owners in the mid-19th century.

Ray Wheeler, the former Technical Director of Westland Aerospace and the author of two books on the history of Saunders-Roe, for the endless suggestions of contacts that could help me.

David Wilkinson, whose knowledge of lifeboats was invaluable and who made the contents of his lifeboat picture collection available to me.

David Reed, David Marshall and Wayne Pritchett, the Harbour Master at Newport, Isle of Wight, as well as the many other members of the Isle of Wight branch of

CONTENTS

the World Ship Society for their continuous help throughout the project.

In addition, the following organisations deserve mention for their generous help: Admiralty Hydrographic Office, Fleet Air Arm Museum, Morgan-Grampian Limited (publishers of *The Engineer* magazine), Royal National Lifeboat Institution, Royal Naval Museum Information Service, Royal Navy Submarine Museum, The Science Museum and the World Ship Photo Library.

Finally, my particular thanks go to my wife Jane who typed the manuscript as well as countless letters and who indulged my absence from duty in the middle of a kitchen refurbishment that had been overdue for more than ten years.

During the shipyard's existence, prior to the period when Ron Trowell was responsible for the official Company photographs, a number of well-known local photographers were regularly commissioned to take pictures of ships or of construction work in the yards. Among these were Beken, Debenham and Kirk whose work deserves mention and recognition here.

Today, the former J. Samuel White & Company archives have been dispersed between a number of individuals as well as the Cowes Maritime Museum and the National Maritime Museum.

In all cases where material is known to have originated from or was commissioned by the Company it has been acknowledged as follows:
White's Archives
White's Archives, Cowes Maritime Museum
White's Archives, Ron Trowell
White's Archives, Wayne Pritchett collection, etc.

BIBLIOGRAPHY

Burns, Lt Cdr K. V. DSM RN *Badges and Battle Honours of HM Ships*

Caws, Sheila, and Brinton, Roy *Cowes and East Cowes - Past and Present* (1983)

Colledge, J. J. *Ships of the Royal Navy*, Volumes 1 & 2

Conway's All the World's Fighting Ships, 1922-1946

Conway's History of the Ship: The Eclipse of the Big Gun - The Warship, 1906-1945 (1992)

Davies, Ken *Solent Passages and Their Steamers* (1982)

Goodall, Michael H. *The Wight Aircraft - The History of the Aviation Department of J. Samuel White and Company Limited, 1913-1919* (1973)

Hocking, Charles *Dictionary of Disasters at Sea During the Age of Steam, 1824-1962* (1969)

Janes Fighting Ships (various)

Lloyds Register of Ships (various)

Lloyds Yacht Register (various)

March, Edgar J. *British Destroyers, 1892-1953* (1966)

Rance, Adrian *Seaplanes and Flying Boats of the Solent*

Tagg, Albert E., and Wheeler, Raymond L. *From Sea to Air - The Heritage of Sam Saunders* (1989)

J. Samuel White & Company Ltd *Shipbuilding: From Smack to Frigate, from Cutter to Destroyer* (1928)
Whites of Cowes, Shipbuilders (1949)

In addition:
Yard lists and unpublished manuscript notes prepared by Raymond F. Sprake
Unpublished notes on White's prepared by Frank C. Bowen

6   MARITIME HERITAGE

INTRODUCTION

As you arrive by sea at Cowes in the north of the Isle of Wight, at the mouth of the River Medina, you cannot fail to notice a prominent landmark dominating the harbour scene. This is the skeletal black frame of the huge hammer-head crane, topped with its box-like winding houses, that towers above the other buildings on the West Cowes river bank.

The crane was first erected in 1911 in the midst of the shipyard that operated there until the late 1960s, and even though the yard has been closed for over 20 years, the crane has remained in operation as a valuable tool serving the smaller boat-building company that now occupies the site.

As a constant reminder of the original shipyard, the crane is now something of a permanent monument to the once great shipbuilding firm of J. Samuel White & Company Limited which was the owner and operator of the shipyard.

The name White stands out above all others in the maritime heritage of Cowes in the Isle of Wight. From its humble beginnings in Kent, the White family shipbuilding concern developed into a large and diverse business following its relocation to Cowes in the early 19th century.

It was around 1803 that Thomas White, grandson of the founder, transferred the shipbuilding business that bore his family name from Broadstairs to the mouth of the River Medina, bringing to the island scene the pioneering and innovative spirit for which he had already established a reputation. This move, based on some shrewd commercial reasoning, seemed at the time to be a relatively minor occurrence outside of the world of maritime affairs. In retrospect, however, it came to have a special significance, representing the nominal birth date of what was later to become recognised as a world leader in the design and construction of small to medium-sized naval and merchant ships.

The business flourished and grew in its new location, partly due to a quite aggressive policy of investment in new facilities and partly through a willingness by the Company to develop and exploit innovative design principles and construction methods. The resulting success contributed greatly to the prosperity of the island community. For the next 150 and more years White's ships, both commercial and naval, acquired an enviable reputation for quality and workmanship. By the end of the Victorian era, White's was already distinguished as the designer and constructor of fast, highly manoeuvrable torpedo boat destroyers for the Royal Navy. In fact, many famous warships were built by White's including HMS *Broke*, HMS *Botha*, HMS *Faulknor* and ORP *Blyskawica*. In the two World Wars the yards' output for the war effort was considered among the highest in Great Britain.

Sadly, after nearly two centuries of expansion, the Company was affected by the general decline in British shipbuilding in the early 1960s. The last ship to be built for the Royal Navy was the frigate HMS *Arethusa*. When she left the yard in 1965, over three centuries of shipbuilding supremacy by White's and its forebears came to an end. In 1981, some time after all shipbuilding activity had closed down, and bearing a different name as a result of an earlier takeover, the Company finally ceased trading.

Over the 178 years of its existence at Cowes, ownership of the firm's various yards was identified by a number of different, sometimes overlapping but equally official titles reflecting various family consortia, the best known being J. Samuel White from 1860 onwards. Irrespective of whichever was the formal Company name at any particular time, the shipyard was always referred to in shipping circles and will always be remembered locally as 'White's of Cowes'. This book is the history of the White's shipyard and the famous marque of ships that were rightfully acclaimed in the Company's slogan 'White's-built, Well-built!'.

Also bearing that slogan, this book is very much a part of the social history of Cowes and the dominant industry which for years provided the main source of employment for its inhabitants. It has been written as a tribute to all those generations of craftsmen whose efforts are recognised in the many excellent products of the shipyard, products which often continued to give good service to their owners long after what may be regarded as typical lifespans. It is hoped that the many former employees of the yard who are still alive will take credit and pleasure from having played an active part in the tradition that is this great Company's past. It is hoped, too, that they and other readers will enjoy a nostalgic trip down Memory Lane as they recall the events described in the later chapters of the book.

This book is also dedicated to the memory of a great enthusiast of the White's shipbuilding tradition, the late Raymond F. Sprake. Ray is fondly remembered as a local lover of ships and shipping affairs, known around the world through his membership of the World Ship Society in which capacity he was a founder member of the Isle of Wight branch. It is to his committed sense of the importance of the White's history as well as to his own extensive research into the shipyard's past that this book owes its inspiration.

In writing the book, I have tried to present a history of White's of Cowes that will be of interest and give pleasure to both the general reader and the shipping enthusiast. For this reason, while I have provided a certain amount of statistical information, notably in the four

Above left The Medina Dock and Shipyard in 1856 - a general view from the River Medina. *White's Archives*

Left The White's shipyard hammer-head crane of 1911 continues to serve the businesses of the Industrial Estate community. Quite large marine craft are still handled by the former shipyard such as the *Seacat Tasmania* shown here undergoing a refit. *David L. Williams*

Appendices, of the warships and lifeboats built and Company-owned vessels, I have quite deliberately avoided over-emphasising this aspect of the content. Instead I have attempted to present this portrait of the White's shipbuilding firm as a social history of the shipyard and a chronology of its development and products. Thus I have not considered it to be critical if a particular speed quoted is incorrect or a given ship's length or armament at a particular time is not precisely stated. Similarly, while I have made every effort to describe ships and events accurately, I cannot claim that the book is infallible in this respect and should not, therefore, need to apologise for any such errors or omissions, as that was not the purpose of this book.

The story of the White's shipyards and the White's-built ships is full of variety and incident. Inevitably, in deciding what should go into the book, something of importance may, regrettably, have been left out. It is a reflection on the richly woven tapestry that is the heritage of this once proud shipbuilding firm that, for every account related here, there are another ten that have gone untold.

White's family tree

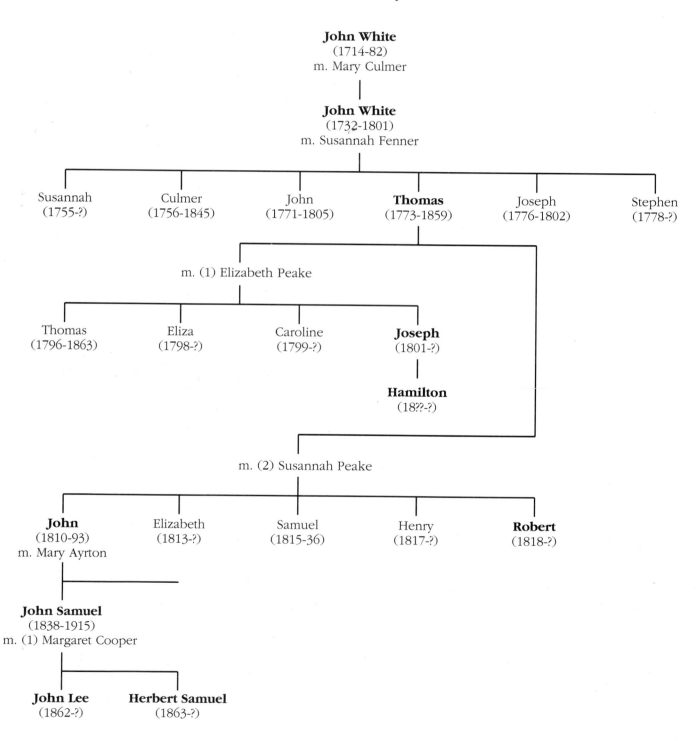

Origins

The early history of the White's family shipbuilding activities at Broadstairs, in the Isle of Thanet, is surrounded by some uncertainty due to the absence of complete or reliable records. As a result, the precise details of that period are now lost in the mists of time and any account of White's formative years must, therefore, depend on a measure of speculation and assumption.

By the time Thomas White (1773-1859) had taken over stewardship of the White family shipbuilding business around 1800, at least three generations of John White - his great-grandfather, his grandfather and his father - had already left their mark as constructors of ships of some renown. By the middle of the 1700s the shipyard at Broadstairs was an established concern building a wide range of vessel types. Besides producing fishing smacks for the local trade, the yard also built fast cutters for the Naval and Revenue services as well as brigantines and a

Some examples of the designs for ships contained in John White's Draft Book, dated 1764. *White's Archives*

number of West Indiamen, including the *Isle of Thanet* which, at around 400 tons burthen, was probably the largest ship ever launched at Broadstairs.

John White (1732-1801) the younger, Thomas's father, published a draft book of hull designs in 1764, some showing quite large and ambitious ships up to the size of frigates. This book, which aroused great interest at the time, is now held by the National Maritime Museum at Greenwich.

Thomas White was John White's third son but, apparently, the only one of five boys to be interested in pursuing the family profession; he eventually took charge of the running of the business around the end of the 18th century. It seems that Thomas was a shrewd businessman and, to use a rather modern idiom, he displayed entrepreneurial flair. He was intelligent and technically astute, genial and philanthropic. Later he showed directorial genius by discreetly masterminding Company policy while allowing each of his sons a measure of independence, permitting them to pursue their separate business interests so as to avoid frustrating their natural energy and enthusiasm for shipbuilding.

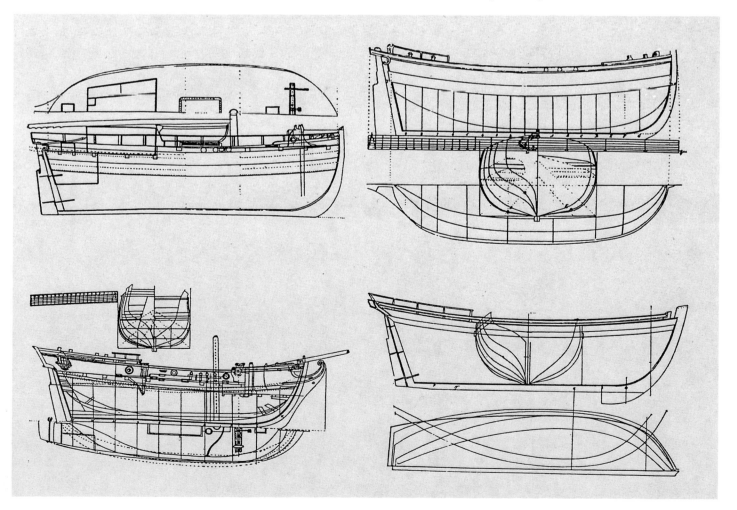

Cowes before White's

Just as there are gaps in the early history of the White family, so, too, a similar shortage of documentary records has left many unanswered questions about the chronology of the former Nye shipyard at Cowes, purchased by White's some time around 1803. In particular there is doubt as to the precise location of the original building ways and the composition of yard facilities, together with the origins and circumstances of several other early Cowes shipbuilders which were functioning at various times during the latter half of the 18th century and which, as a result of their association with the Nye Yard, form part of White's ancestry. Nye was almost certainly the founder of the yard, but long after he had vacated the premises himself it continued to be known by his name even though it was occupied by other proprietors.

Admiralty records indicate that by 1800 the Nye yard had established a proud reputation as a builder of vessels for the Royal Navy. Naval construction had begun with Nye himself in the 32-gun fifth rate line of battleship HMS *Poole*, launched on 6 August 1696. She was followed by HMS *Jersey*, a 48-gun fourth rate line of battleship launched on 24 November 1698. As a result of the continuation by White's of the warship-building tradition commenced by Nye, the Company was to earn the ultimate distinction of being the oldest private shipyard on the Admiralty List, being represented for some 264 years.

The Nye shipyard was situated on the eastern shore of the River Medina, somewhere just south of the present-day floating-bridge terminus at East Cowes where a small tributary joined the main waterway. Apparently ships were launched into a dredged channel alongside two building berths. As to the lifting and workshop facilities, unfortunately little is now known.

By the time of the acquisition by White's, the occupants of Nye's shipyard had already changed more than once. Here, too, the evidence is sketchy, but naval and local records indicate that in 1745 Philemon Ewer took over ownership of the yard and that between then and 1850 it was productive under his name. During this time HMS *Vanguard* was constructed for the Navy, the third ship of the name and the largest ship built on the River Medina up to that time. Launched on 16 April 1748, of 1,419 tons burthen, she was a 70-gun third rate line of battleship.

Later, Ewer leased the yard to Robert Fabian. Between 1775 and 1790 Fabian and his son built some equally famous ships, including the 64-gun third raters HMS *Repulse* and HMS *Veteran*, launched, respectively, on 28 November 1780 and 14 August 1787. Fabian's shipbuilding partnership was dissolved in 1792, and five years later, on the death of Philemon Ewer, the disposal of the shipyard was decreed by his will. It is uncertain whether anyone else occupied the yard in the five years before the arrival of White's.

Early years at Cowes

Despite the incoherency of the White Company's historical background on the Isle of Wight during this embryonic period, enough is known to demonstrate that it inherited a worthy pedigree that extended back more than a hundred years. When the Nye yard came on to the market in 1802, Thomas White was quick to purchase it, completely closing down the Broadstairs operation and moving his family - wife Elizabeth, sons Thomas and Joseph, and daughters Eliza and Caroline - down to Cowes.

No doubt a number of factors influenced the move from Broadstairs to Cowes, with all the upheaval that this involved for both the business and the family. Thomas White considered naval work to be vital for the future of the business and, although the nearby Chatham dockyard offered the Broadstairs-based concern attractive prospects for warship construction, the fact was that Portsmouth was the home of the Royal Navy and most naval work was concentrated there. Being close to Portsmouth Dockyard allowed the business to keep in intimate touch with naval affairs, permitting the development of closer contacts with the Admiralty.

Even had Thomas White secured the level of orders at Broadstairs to which he aspired, the size of warships was then growing fast and the limits of draught on the northeast Kent coastline imposed restrictions on the maximum size of vessel that could be launched. No such impediment existed on the River Medina where it was possible to launch vessels significantly larger than those already in service.

In addition, a sufficiently large and ready-skilled workforce was already employed in the existing Cowes shipyards and the nearby New Forest and Parkhurst Forests offered a convenient and abundant source of oak for the construction of the exclusively wooden-hulled ships of the day.

The arrival of the White family brought a dynamic spirit and energy to the former Nye shipyard, reflected in the ambitious plans for the expansion of the shipbuilding activities beyond what was then the limits of its capability. Having said that, for many years after the takeover Thomas White was content to turn out small vessels along the lines of those that had been produced by the Company while back in Kent, the first being the 10-gun revenue cutter *Speedwell*. On reflection, even this appears to have been part of Thomas White's grand strategy, for it provided a dependable 'bread and butter' income from which the planned enlargement of the yard's facilities could be financed.

These formative years at Cowes, between 1803 and Thomas White's death in 1859, were critical to the future well-being of the Company. It was through this half century that all the major yard developments were realised, establishing the features that were still fundamentally recognisable in the modern shipyard of the 20th century, and providing all the means that were to be put to such productive benefit in future periods.

The first ten years at Cowes was a period of consolidation, characterised by family rather than business developments. Thomas White married for the second time, following the death of his first wife, and thereafter commenced to have a new family. The first born was John in 1810. Three children later, in 1818, Robert, his last child, was born. John and Robert, together with their older stepbrother, Joseph, represented the emerging second generation of management of the White's concern at Cowes and

Above Model of a two-deck fourth rate line of battleship from 1691, typical of HMS *Jersey*, built by the Nye shipyard, East Cowes, in 1698. *National Maritime Museum*

Right This map, one of the earliest of Cowes, drawn by Lt Murdoch Mackenzie in 1783, shows the Nye shipyard in East Cowes, captioned as 'Two Building Slips for Men of War'. *Admiralty Hydrographic Office*

Below HMS *Vanguard*, a third rate line of battleship of 1,419 tons designed by Sir Jacob Ackworth. The *Vanguard* was started in November 1744 and delivered on 16 April 1748. *White's Archives*

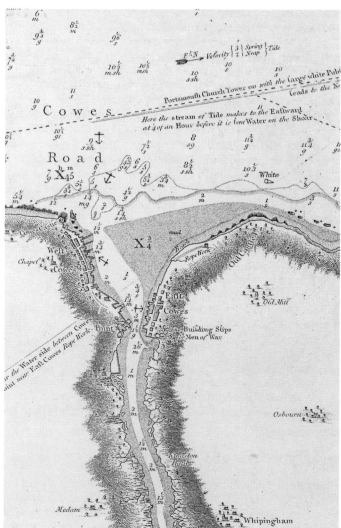

all three entered the business at an early age, assisting their father in the realisation of his plans, each in his individual way.

Joseph White's specialisation was yacht design and construction, and for many years he was regarded, unofficially, as the preferred designer and builder for the members of the Royal Yacht Squadron. In addition, the origins of the clipper ship have been attributed to him, although this cannot now be confirmed or refuted.

John White also became a designer, but the application of his skills extended into the science of ship dynamics, for he was anxious to establish the performance of vessels before they were built by testing clockwork scale models.

Robert, who was to partner John in the building of lifeboats, was essentially a practical shipbuilder. He was a great innovator who derived his inspiration from the emerging technology of the steam age. He invented and patented a number of new ship construction techniques as well as several mechanical appliances that were employed in the shipyard.

The Thetis Yard

Initially, while his sons were growing, Thomas White ran the firm alone. His first major venture was the construction of the Thetis Yard in West Cowes which was officially opened on 1 October 1815. The new shipyard was erected on reclaimed marshland, adjacent to the former main office building of J. Samuel White's which is still standing in Medina Road.

The Thetis Yard established Thomas White's business for the first time on both sides of the River Medina. Among its features was a drydock capable of taking ships of up to 800 tons burthen, as the primary workload of the yard was to be repairs although new construction would also be undertaken.

The drydock was the only non-Naval dock in a large area and it had been built with repairs to London-bound East Indiamen in mind, in competition with the Thames repair yards. This was a most ambitious investment for the future, coming more than 20 years before Southampton started to open up as a port for international shipping, a development which would have virtually guaranteed a healthy level of repair and overhaul business. In the event, both shipping and shipbuilding interests on the River Thames combined to inhibit the level of repair work that transferred to White's at Cowes and, as a consequence, the Thetis Dock was not altogether the success that had been hoped. By the time the port of Southampton was established as a major centre of shipping, in the mid-1800s, the Thetis Dock was already too small to handle the vessels of the day, a matter which prompted Thomas White to commission a larger replacement.

The Falcon and Medina Yards

Joseph White had not yet reached his 20th year but already he was working in his father's business in a position of responsibility - Thomas White evidently had immense confidence in his son's ability despite his rela-

tive inexperience. Joseph's aptitude was rewarded with the opportunity to mastermind the next important expansion of the building facilities on the East Cowes waterfront. This culminated in the opening of the Falcon Yard in 1825 for the building of yachts. Joseph was permitted to run this as a partially separate business venture.

The Falcon Yard took its name from the Earl of Yarborough's brigantine yacht *Falcon* which had been built by Thomas White in 1815. As the new yard expanded outwards into the River Medina, on reclaimed land, and along the shoreline, it progressively encompassed, absorbed and incorporated the original Nye Yard. Eventually all trace of the original Nye Yard had disappeared.

During the years in which the Thetis Dock and Falcon Yard were under development, Thomas White was also engaged in constructing yet another new shipyard on the West Cowes side of the River Medina. Until the early 19th century, this area, which directly faced the Falcon Yard, had been tidal marshland partly used as salterns, pools along the river's edge for the natural evaporation of sea water to produce salt. Early on, Thomas White built a family house in this area set amidst spacious gardens. It was in these gardens that John White built his open-air test tank for experimental work on model ships. Later the first building slips were erected along the river frontage, permitting vessels to be launched into the river from both shores. The shipbuilding complex that gradually emerged in this area was known as the Medina or West Cowes Shipyard.

Yacht construction, East Cowes

Joseph White built numerous speedy and successful racing yachts at the Falcon Yard in the years that followed, as well as many fast cutters for the Royal Navy. Most notable of the vessels built in this period was the brigantine yacht *Waterwitch*, commissioned by the Earl of Belfast as a development of the *Louisa* built in 1828 and launched at East Cowes on 18 June 1832. Of 331 tons with dimensions of 90 feet length and 29 feet beam, the *Waterwitch* disputes with Andrew Hall's *Scottish Maid* of 1839 the claim of being the first true clipper ship in the world; she apparently possessed the clipper ship's characteristic feature of a hollow bow at the waterline. Unfortunately, authentic plans of the *Waterwitch* no longer exist as evidence by which this claim could be substantiated. But whether or not she was the first clipper, the *Waterwitch* was a most successful craft, strongly built as well as fast and manoeuvrable, and her many racing contests, in which she soundly beat all her contemporaries, aroused bitter rivalry and not a little jealousy.

The *Waterwitch* had been designed as an improvement to the standard design of 10-gun naval brig, a type then bitterly criticised in naval circles. In 1834 she was purchased by the Royal Navy to operate in a squadron of other brigs of competitive designs in order to evaluate their performance in competition with each other. In the course of this she confirmed her total superiority, an outcome that compelled a statement in Parliament that the ships designed by others 'must be given the bows of Mr Joseph White's vessels'.

The Thetis Dock in 1845, showing a ship in drydock and other craft on slipways at various stages of construction. *White's Archives*

One of the most celebrated of the early ships built by White's was the 20-ton brig *Waterwitch*, completed in 1834. Claimed as the first vessel with clipper bow lines, her introduction heralded important improvements to naval brigs. *White's Archives*

The official opening of the Medina Steam Frigate Dock in March 1845. P&O's *Braganza* is shown already berthed in the new drydock. *Illustrated London News*

The famous little ship gave valiant and constant service to the Navy, operating mainly off the coast of West Africa, intercepting and capturing slave ships, until she was disposed of in 1861. When, in 1843, the *Waterwitch* required repairs, Joseph White offered to take on the contract for the work at a price that was half that estimated by the Portsmouth Dockyard. Hauled up on the patent slip at the Falcon Yard, the repairs took just under a year, and her second launching, in June 1844, was attended by as large and enthusiastic a crowd as that which had witnessed the first launch ten years earlier.

During the period from 1835 to 1859, the White's family business comprised a number of different enterprises operating on the river front, each of which represented different consortia between the various members of the family. This is quite a confused period and it is difficult to say with any degree of certainty which enterprises or partnerships were functioning at which precise times. An impression of the diversity of these many and various concerns can be obtained from contemporary newspaper reports as well as advertisements and entries in trade gazetteers.

John White had entered the business around the late 1820s, followed by his brother Robert some time during the next ten years. All the key players who controlled the fortunes of the collective shipbuilding businesses over the next quarter of a century were now in place. The following list is a summary of the constituent White family companies over this first half century or so:

East Cowes   *ca* 1803-1825 Thomas White, former Nye Yard
             ca 1825-1855 Joseph White, Falcon Yard
             ca 1855-1860 Hamilton White (son of Joseph), Falcon Yard

West Cowes   ca 1815-1820 Thomas White, Thetis Yard
             ca 1820-1830 Thomas White, Thetis Yard
                and Medina Shipyard
             ca 1830-1845 Thomas White, Thetis Yard
             ca 1830-1845 John White, Medina Shipyard
             ca 1845-1860 Thomas & John White, Thetis
                Yard, Medina Dock and Medina Shipyard
             ca 1845-1860 John & Robert White, lifeboat
                yard West Cowes

The ships built through this period continued to be mainly cutters, brigs and schooners of varying sizes, the majority being for the revenue service. The most distinctive of these was the revenue cutter *Vulcan* constructed in 1834, only the third steam-propelled vessel built by White's. White's first steam-driven craft had been another *Falcon*, a paddle steamer, built in 1817. She was followed by the paddle steamer *Duke of Buccleuch* in 1830.

At 325 tons, the *Vulcan* was double the size of the largest sailing cutters then in service, providing the revenue service with a huge margin of superiority. Like the other early steam vessels built by the Company, she was not engined at White's because, at that time, the yards did not have their own engine shop.

In 1838 John Samuel White was born, the first son of John. John Samuel, or J. Samuel as he was known, was to have the most profound influence on the future fortunes of the shipbuilding business. During his lifetime and under his leadership, the various individual enterprises were to be consolidated into a single, powerful Company which was to acquire, develop and sustain an enviable reputation for building first-class, high-speed warships.

The Medina Drydock

Back when J. Samuel was still only six, a further major expansion of the shipyard facilities was set in train. This was the start of the construction of the Medina Drydock or, as it was then known, the Medina Steam Frigate Dock. Work started in April 1844 alongside the existing shipyard.

The foundations of the dock was almost a solid mass of bearers extending across the dock's width, set in concrete resting on blue slipper clay which, as revealed by borings, extended to a depth of 200 feet below the dock bottom. The dock heads consisted of massive piers and wing walls built of huge blocks of Portland stone which were also erected on concrete foundations. The ends of the wing walls extended 100 feet out into the river in the form of stages or platforms on either side of the entrance gates. Alongside the dock an engine house was built containing powerful steam-driven pumps for emptying the dock.

Viewed from above, as well as in section, the dock was shaped to resemble the hull of a ship. It was 257 feet in extreme length and 62 feet in breadth. The entrance was sufficiently wide to admit the largest steam vessels then in service without the necessity to unship their paddle wheels. The depth of water over the dock sill was 16 feet on spring tides and 13 feet on neap tides; this allowed White's to handle large naval ships, up to the size of 74-gun line of battleships, a frequent occurrence when Portsmouth Dockyard's repair facilities were burdened beyond their capacity.

Again, Thomas White was bidding to secure repair work which would otherwise be diverted to the River Thames, there being no other comparable commercial facility along the entire length of the Channel coast in those days.

This time, however, the target was also the luxury mail packets operating out of Southampton. In 1841 White's had established a link with the Royal West India Mail Steam Packet Company, later the Royal Mail Line, by securing the contract to build the 1,800-ton wooden paddle steamer *Medina*. Fitted with side lever engines built by Edward Bury of Liverpool, the *Medina* was launched on 6 July 1841 and commenced her maiden voyage in January of the following year.

In 1844 a similar association was forged with another of the prominent ship owners based in Southampton. On this occasion it was the Peninsular & Oriental Steamship Company (P&O) whose *Braganza* was taken in hand for lengthening by the insertion of a 30-foot-long midships section. The *Braganza* was hauled up on White's patent slip in the Medina Shipyard for the execution of the work. Coincidentally, the vessel returned to Cowes for a refit during the following year at the time of the opening of the Medina Dock in March 1845, thus becoming the first vessel to enter the new dock.

Two further smaller graving docks were completed in the years immediately following the commissioning of the Medina Dock. Together the various docks now available to White's for repair work were kept well employed, especially on work for the Royal Navy. Once again, however, events had overtaken White's on the commercial side. On 27 July 1846 the first and largest of three new drydocks was opened at Southampton. With a length of 400 feet it immediately surpassed by a significant margin the capacity of the Medina Dock. By 1854 all three of Southampton's drydocks were operational and, to White's disadvantage, they were soon in regular use by the Royal Mail and P&O companies' ships. For the time being at least, the Medina Dock was kept busy but the writing was on the wall and inside half a century all four of White's drydocks had gone, closed and filled in.

Meanwhile the yard's building activities continued apace with more, largely indistinctive vessels leaving the yards, mainly brigs and schooners. Two of these ships are perhaps worthy of mention, however. The 12-ton brig *Contest* was completed for the Royal Navy in 1846, a further development of the *Waterwitch* and the *Daring*, the latter having been built by Portsmouth Dockyard to Joseph White's designs. The year 1846 also witnessed the completion of the Czar's schooner yacht *Victoria* at the Falcon Yard. Prior to her departure for St Petersburg she was inspected by Queen Victoria and Prince Albert, possibly the first occasion on which a Royal party visited the shipyard.

Patent lifeboat construction, West Cowes

Around 1845, John and Robert White established their lifeboat-building yard in West Cowes. In collaboration with a neighbour, Andrew Lamb, they had designed a new type of self-righting lifeboat based on whaler principles with airtight compartments along each side and at each end, rather than just over the gunwales. Patented as the Lamb & White Lifeboat, it formed the basis of White's lifeboat-building output until the construction of RNLI-designed craft commenced in earnest in the early 1920s. The Lamb & White boats were carvel built and, though they carried no ballast, they were not as prone to capsizing as ordinary self-righters.

The boats were available in a number of variants - a 27-foot-long whaleboat, a 30-foot-long lifeboat, as supplied to the Royal Yacht *Victoria & Albert* and to the P&O and Royal Mail Steamship Companies, a clench-built lifeboat gig, a lifeboat cutter and, ultimately, 25-foot and 32-foot-long versions of the improved patent lifeboat.

These lifeboats were supplied to a wide range of customers and countries, and the list of testimonials was impressive - from the Emperors of Russia and France, the Dutch Royal Navy and the Governments of Portugal, Turkey, Egypt and New Zealand, to name but a few.

The Lamb & White patent lifeboat was designed and mainly intended for shipboard service, but it attracted the attention of shore life-saving stations and was increasingly ordered for this role. The first to be supplied was one of the 27-foot boats for St Dogmeals, Cardiganshire, in 1849. Thomas White presented the lifeboat *Mary White* to the Broadstairs lifeboat station, establishing a special patronage with the White family's town of origin. In 1851 the *Culmer White* was donated for service at the same station, and in 1855 she was further supplemented by the *Dreadnought*. Over the years that followed, many more Lamb & White lifeboats were adopted by other independent stations. A number of the stations of the National Shipwreck Institution (NSI), later the Royal National Lifeboat Institution (RNLI), also took delivery of patent lifeboats, though this was not a widespread experience, as an Institution committee had assessed the Lamb & White craft rather unfavourably. Nevertheless, later, on the formation of the RNLI, all these lifeboats, from both independent and NSI stations, formed part of the RNLI's original fleet list.

When in 1860 the Coastguard Service was transferred under the control of the Admiralty, over 100 existing gigs were replaced by 27-foot life-whaleboats stationed around the coasts of England, Scotland and Ireland.

Following the disastrous loss of a Royal Navy ship, the Admiralty directed that every one of its vessels should be fitted with suitable lifeboats, and 500 Lamb & White patent lifeboats were ordered to fulfil this requirement.

The unfolding years of the early Victorian era were exciting years, marked by the introduction of other innovative construction practices and increasingly interesting vessels. The Company was contracted to build some of the first paddle steamships for the Ottoman (Turkish) Navy, among them the *Vasita-I-Ticaret*, launched in September 1847, and the *Medar-I-Ticaret* and *Nümayis Ticaret*, launched simultaneously on 18 March of the same year. All these ships were fitted with 250 hp Maudslay engines.

In 1852 White's built one of the seven original wooden paddle ferries of the Southampton & Isle of Wight Company, later the Southampton, Isle of Wight & South of England Royal Mail Steam Packet Company and today styled as the Red Funnel Group. Started as *The Times* but not completed, the unengined vessel was acquired as a bare hull and finished for her new owners in 1862 as the *Medina*. Measuring 104 gross tons and 121 feet in length by 15 feet beam, she was employed on the regular service to the Isle of Wight as well as on excursions along the south coast. When the *Great Eastern* was moored off Weymouth, the *Medina* made special trips around her carrying sightseers eager to catch a glimpse of this marine giant.

Patent diagonal construction system

Prompted by P&O, whose ships suffered extensively from dry rot in the curved timbers of the frame caused by foul bilge air getting trapped in between, necessitating frequent and extensive repairs, John and Robert White began to investigate the possibilities of building ships in a way that would permit the reduction of the normal multiplicity of frame timbers. The desired result was accomplished by the retention of only the floors and lower futtocks as a foundation, with the upper part of the hull completed by means of diagonal and longitudinal planking, a system which John White had patented.

Though the system devised by the Whites was not the first diagonal method of construction, it was a significant improvement on all the earlier approaches and, in conjunction with a deeper keel, gave enormous superiority in strength, buoyancy and capacity. In addition, watertight bulkheads could be installed in White's diagonal-built ships very much more easily and efficiently than in ships with normal frame timbers. The original objective of improved durability and reduced need for repairs was also fully realised by the system although the initial costs of construction of diagonal-built ships were somewhat higher.

The Admiralty expressed considerable interest in the White patent diagonal system of construction because the sides of naval ships built by this method would be able to support more armour. Nevertheless, no naval orders were received prior to the Crimean War. It fell to P&O and Royal Mail to demonstrate faith in John White's innovative system by ordering, respectively, the packet steamers *Tartar* and *Vectis* on the one hand, and the *Solent* on the other, all built by the patent diagonal method of planking.

Though small by today's standards, these were prestigious, first-rate ships of their time, the combined order as well as its source marking an important milestone in the growing recognition and wider acclaim for the quality output of the White's yards. Collectively the three ships represented the major part of the West Cowes shipyard's production for 1853.

The *Tartar*, first of the three, was chartered by the Navy for service in the Far East. Later, in 1855, she was purchased outright and renamed HMS *Coromandel*. Royal Mail's *Solent* was the largest vessel to be built on the diagonal system, measuring 310 feet in overall length with a gross tonnage of 2,230; the Medina Drydock had to be lengthened in order to accommodate her for coppering.

The launch of the *Vectis* on 11 January 1853 turned out

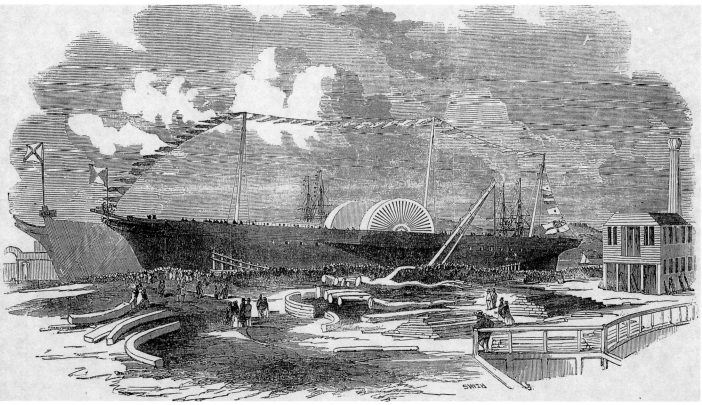

to be Thomas White's last public involvement in the affairs of the shipyard. He was already in semi-retirement, at 80 years of age, having handed over practically the whole of the management of the West Cowes facilities to his sons John and Robert over the preceding years. Appropriately enough, Thomas christened the *Vectis* with the words 'Success to the first of the new school'. Thereafter Thomas retired from all active participation in the business and, with the exception of the Falcon Yard, the yards now came under the control of John White.

Other notable ships built on White's patented diagonal

Top The Turkish Navy's paddle steamship *Vasita-I-Ticaret*. National Maritime Museum

Above On the slipway just prior to her launch on 11 January 1853 is the P&O paddle steam packet *Vectis*. In the background is Royal Mail's *Solent*. The *Vectis*'s 400 hp engines were constructed by Messrs John Penn & Company. Robert White had hoped that the patented diagonal planking construction method used for the *Tartar*, *Solent* and *Vectis* would forestall the trend towards iron-built craft. However, the outbreak of the Crimean War interrupted progress with the development of the diagonal principle, after which iron-hulled ships were preferred to wooden-hulled vessels. *Illustrated London News*

principle included the 140-ton clipper schooner *Royal Blue Jacket*, finished for Ivens & Chessel of Bristol in 1854, and the full-rigged ship *Heroes of Alma* built for Shepherds in 1855 for their Far East service.

At this time the demands of the Crimean War were imposing themselves on the shipyard. White's was kept fully occupied on both repair work and the construction of new, shallow-draught gunboats for the Royal Navy.

The Admiralty requested White's to undertake even more work, but the Company was already employing all the skilled shipwrights in the area. Gas lighting had been introduced into the shipyard to permit the introduction of a nightwork shift to increase production, but to have taken on these additional orders would have resulted in either late deliveries or inferior work, neither of which White's was prepared to entertain as they conflicted with the Company's expressed policy. The extra work was consequently declined, demonstrating a lack of compromise over standards that on more than one occasion led to disagreements between White's and the Admiralty.

Foreign orders

Between 1850 and 1860 a number of interesting developments occurred. In 1855 the yard completed its last opium clipper for Dent & Company. This was the *Wild Dayrell*, generally regarded as the fastest and best known in the trade. As one line of business was closing, however, other new opportunities were emerging. From the outset White's had supplied the occasional vessel to foreign owners, but the 1850s saw the Company commence the pursuit of export business with greater intent. A sequence of large overseas orders was secured, involving a total of 27 ships built between 1853 and 1860.

The lead ship was the paddle steamer *Rumeli* for Sirketi-Hayriye (the Bosphorus Steam Navigation Company). She was followed by five more ferries for the same owners, being the *Tarabya*, *Göksu*, *Beylerbeyi*, *Tophane* and *Besiktas*. These ships measured 188 gross tons and were fitted with Maudslay engines. Four years later a second group of paddle ferries were constructed for Serketi-Hayriye. This group of five vessels comprised the *Beykoz*, *Sariyer*, *Istinye*, *Mirgun* and *Anadolu*, which, at 288 gross tons, were significantly larger than the first batch. The Turkish owners must surely have been well satisfied with the ships built for them by White's, for they returned to the Company for a further quantity of four ferry boats in 1860, these being the *Kabatas*, *Galata*, *Buyukdere* and *Beyazid*. Of varying dimensions, these ships were fitted with either Maudslay or Penn engines.

Simultaneously, on the naval side, the despatch vessels *Appa* and *Princeza de Joinville* were built for the Brazilian Navy. They measured 927 tons and 198 feet in overall length. Next came a group of support ships for the Turkish Navy, two unnamed tugs in 1853, followed by the 484-ton paddle supply ships *Kilic Ali* (ex-*Constantinople*) and *Hayreddin* (ex-*Danube*) and the storeships *Oltanica* (ex-*Golden Horn*) and *Catalca* (ex-*Sweet Water*). The latter pair were the first screw-propelled ships built by White's, with engines supplied by Summers & Day of Southampton.

The Turkish order was completed with three corvettes, which were to form part of a Black Sea squadron mandated by the Treaty of Paris in settlement of the Crimean War, and a small schooner-rigged gunboat named the *Akka*. The corvettes were the *Seddül Bahir*, of 609 tons and 174 feet in length, and the 780-ton sister vessels *Sinop* and *Izmir*, all of which were delivered by British crews in 1860. These barque-rigged vessels were fitted with Humphrys-built engines driving a single screw in each case. So well did all these vessels perform that in 1868 the Turkish Navy returned to White's with another order for a fleet of small ships, commencing with the auxiliary *Sahir*.

The supply of first-rate naval vessels to foreign governments continued to be a mainstay of White's shipbuilding business culminating in the design and construction of a number of distinctive destroyer classes during the 20th century. These superior warships of the future owed their existence to another significant development in the affairs of the White's shipyards that dated from around the late 1850s.

By this time John Samuel White was also in harness with the Company. He was immediately involved on the designing side, one of his early activities being the development of an improved type of steam launch for the Royal Navy. The examples which had already been supplied to the fleet were notorious for their unreliable performance and lack

of seaworthiness. Though John Samuel's efforts seemed of little importance at the time, they were ultimately to lead on to the long line of torpedo boats and destroyers for which White's is now justly famous, a story which was to unfold over the next half century.

The end of the 1850s turned out to be a major milestone in the history of the White company, in effect the closing of one era and the opening of another. Thomas White died in 1859, aged 86 years, mourned by the family and the workforce alike. Though he had been retired for some time he was genuinely popular in the shipyard, having been a gentleman of the 'old school', imbued with a philanthropic responsibility for the men who toiled on his and his sons' behalf. At this time, when the town's population had grown to approximately 10,000, anything between 500 and 1,000 men were regularly employed in the combined shipyards, according to the level of business in hand.

The Medina Shipyard in 1859, with HMS *Carnatic* under repair in the drydock. *White's Archives*

Wooden ships-of-war building at Cowes in the late 1850s. *White's Archives*

Below The Imperial Chinese paddle despatch vessel *Keang Soo*, built by John White in 1860. Powered by 300 hp engines by Day & Company of Southampton, she achieved a maximum speed of 17 knots over the measured mile in Stokes Bay. Renamed *Kasuga*, she later became the private yacht of the Japanese Shogun, before serving for a period with the Imperial Japanese Navy. She was scrapped in 1898. *Illustrated London News*

2. EMERGENCE AND DOMINANCE OF JOHN SAMUEL WHITE

A new era, a new name

Thomas White's passing coincided with a change of ownership of the East Cowes Falcon Yard. In 1854 Joseph White's concern had suffered a serious financial collapse and he was adjudged to be bankrupt. This reversal of fortunes had been caused by the growing competition from the many other specialist yacht-builders opening up along both shores of the Medina. Since then the day-to-day administration of the Falcon Yard had been the responsibility of Hamilton White, Joseph's son. From 1860 the Falcon Yard started to operate as J. Samuel White, inaugurating the period which was to witness the expansion and growth of White's into a Company of truly international stature and importance.

Of course, this change of ownership also represented a remarkable achievement for the young John Samuel, still only 22 years of age, with his name already 'up in lights', so to speak. It was, however, to be another 24 years until his name was to be proudly displayed above the yards on both sides of the River Medina. In the meanwhile the West Cowes shipyard, the main business, continued under the name and management of his father.

An important change associated with this change of control was the introduction of an official yard list. This identified the majority of the vessels built by the Company from this date, although a number of ships were still built without yard numbers, and some repair work is not included in the list either. Commencing from 1864, yard number 1 was a 25-foot diagonal lifeboat for the Imperial Ottoman Navy.

Steam engines and steam launches

In line with other shipbuilders and engineers of the day, John Samuel White aspired to have more efficient steam engines to fit in the launches that he was developing for naval use. He was equally conscious of a fundamental shortcoming of the shipyards at Cowes through not having an in-plant engine works. He could not address both these deficiencies immediately and, seeing the need for a suitable very high-speed steam engine as being the higher priority, he began to carry out experiments in the Falcon Yard in 1864, in conjunction with the Birmingham engineer George E. Belliss.

Belliss had been working on improvements to steam engines for over a decade and his ideas found a fertile imagination in the mind of the young John Samuel. They were soon able to produce engines running at 500 to 600 rpm and, within three years, Belliss's improved engines were being routinely installed in White's craft, the first being the small screw yacht *Ethel*. Others followed in some quantity. The bigger ships built at West Cowes continued to be fitted with engines built by Maudslay, Day, Penn and others.

John Samuel was impressed by what had been achieved but was still far from satisfied. He could see the

The Thetis Dock and slipways seen in 1863. Next to Thetis House in the centre is the Bell Inn, which still exists and which remained, until quite recently, a licensed premises. In front of the Bell Inn is the Vectis Tower, now the site of the Ticket Office for the Cowes chain ferry on the West Cowes side. *White's Archives*

General view of the West Cowes shipyards in 1866. At the top is the Thetis Dock across Medina Road, now part of a general cargo wharf. An extension to the Company's main office building on Brunswick Place was built on the site of the Falcon Inn, after Second World War bomb damage (see the illustration on page 62). The Medina Dock, lying alongside the present-day Thetis Road, is shown as enlarged to take the packet steamer *Solent*. The Point Shipbuilding Yard, just south of the floating bridge terminus, was absorbed by White's in the 1890s. At the bottom of the map can be seen Thomas White's house and the model testing pond (see the illustration on page 14). *Courtesy of Ordnance Survey (redrawn by D. L. Williams)*

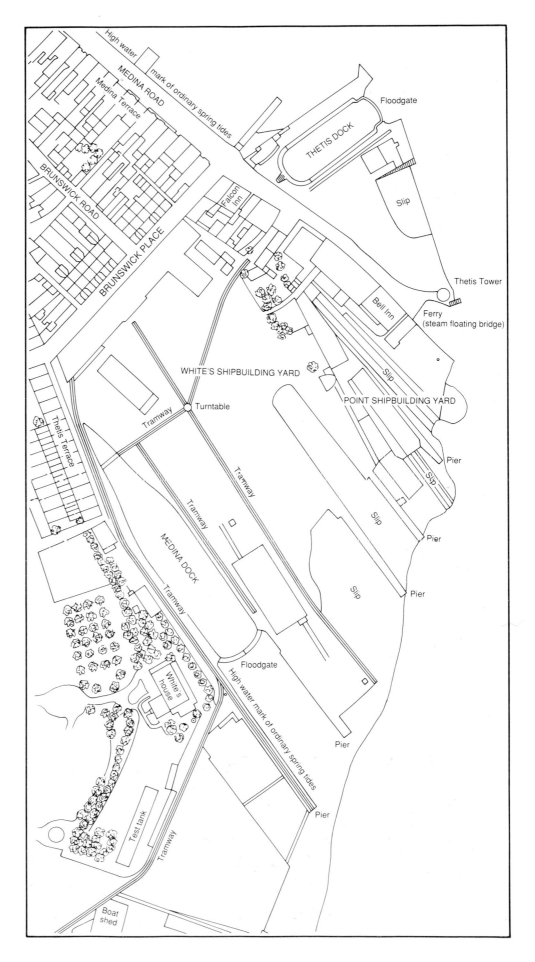

benefits of steam propulsion for so many other applications, limited only by the need for compactness and a good ratio of power output to weight. He planned to fit steam engines in the Lamb & White patent shipboard lifeboats, the first of which was completed for the Marquis of Hastings's private yacht in 1867. In connection with his continuing development of the steam launch, John Samuel also extended a daring offer to the Royal Navy, to build for them at his own expense a steam pinnace which he claimed would beat all existing steam boats in commission with the Service.

At that time typical naval steam launches were between 42 and 45 feet in length and powered by machinery weighing over 4 tons. They had a nominal maximum speed of 9.5 knots, although 7.5 to 8 knots was more typical, and burned 6 lbs of coal per hp per hour. White's offered to build a 36-foot life-pinnace whose machinery would weigh less than 2 tons and which would be capable of steaming at 8 knots more economically. Power for this vessel was supplied by a simple non-condensing steam engine with two cylinders, the steam being supplied by a horizontal boiler; the engine drove a single, four-bladed propeller.

Subsequently a 48-foot steam cutter was built with twin

Left HMS *Euridyce* in the Medina Drydock in 1876. The tower in the background is an extension to Thomas White's house, constructed by John White. Apparently, it had a huge barometer attached to it so that the yard workers could be kept aware of imminent weather changes. *White's Archives*

Right Another view of HMS *Euridyce*, showing her moored outside the drydock. The photograph is dated 17 March 1876. The *Euridyce* was lost in a freak storm in Sandown Bay on 24 March 1878 while returning to Portsmouth from a voyage to the West Indies. It is said that the sea in the vicinity of the accident is now haunted. *White's Archives*

Below This unusual craft is a duck punt, specially constructed for Hamilton White in about 1899. It would be interesting to know the size of the species of duck that warranted such a large gun. The tower of White's house can again be seen. *White's Archives*

screws, capable of attaining speeds of up to 12.5 knots, a record for naval steam launches. The next improvement, again produced in collaboration with George Belliss, was an extremely light, inverted compound condenser engine fitted with a special furnace for forced draught in conjunction with a closed stokehold.

It was to be a few more years before the full combination would be achieved of the sea-keeping qualities of the Lamb & White lifeboat with the strength of the diagonal planking method of construction and the benefits of high-speed steam propulsion. For now, the primary objective remained to secure orders for naval steam launches.

Something of a breakthrough with the Royal Navy had occurred in 1861 when a steam launch was constructed for HMS *Sylvia* for survey work on the West African coast. During trials the launch proved impossible to capsize, remaining afloat even when filled with water. In service it proved to be a good little workhorse that never suffered breakdowns.

The Admiralty was impressed, to say the least, and although typically taciturn in converting this enthusiasm into more orders, this undoubtedly marked the beginning of a long and bountiful association with the Royal Navy in the evolution of these craft.

Already the success of White's shipboard steam launches was attracting orders from foreign navies for craft of this type for employment as patrol vessels, vedettes or second-class torpedo boats.

From 1864, in association with Captain Hire of the Admiralty Transport Service, John White developed a Lifeboat Bridge to facilitate the launching of lifeboats from either side of a ship in an emergency. The design, patented in 1866 as the Hire & White's Lifeboat Bridge, provided for the conversion of part of a ship's bridge into launching ways which could be canted to an angle of 20 degrees, to port or starboard as necessary, allowing lifeboats to be rapidly launched clear of the ship's sides. The apparatus was designed to accommodate 40-foot-long lifeboats with a capacity for 150 to 200 men. By this arrangement all davit and deck stowage of lifeboats could be eliminated.

The naval transport *Orontes* was the first vessel to be fitted with the Lifeboat Bridge. The famous P&O *Himalaya* of 1853 was adapted likewise, as were the other large Indian transports and Government troopships.

All this time the shipyards had been continuing to produce a wide variety of ships and boats in prolific quantities - small sail coasters, schooners, cutters, paddle ferries, steam yachts - all of which helped to maintain full employment. It is impossible to describe all these vessels here, or even make individual reference to them. Among the more interesting that are worthy of mention were the wooden paddle steamer *Vectis*, the first vessel to be ordered and specially built for the Southampton & Isle of Wight Royal Mail Steam Packet Company. She entered service in 1866, engaged on the cross-Solent passenger-carrying schedules and excursion work that ranged from Brighton to Weymouth. There was also the wooden paddle tug *Grinder* that displaced 500 tons and measured 120 feet by 25 feet and which was continuously employed in Portsmouth Dockyard for many years.

The yawl yacht *Latona was* built in 1875 for Mr A. B. Rowley to the designs of W. Fife. She was a particular success story, winning many long-distance and cross-Channel races. In her first season she took 14 first and four second prizes. The following year she completed a classic series of races in competition with the *Florinda*, another outstanding racing yacht of the day that had been rebuilt specially, and she was awarded eight firsts and six second places.

When building work was slack, which was not often, the Company took on the scrapping of surplus warships for the Admiralty. There was also the continuing demand for naval repair work which tended to come in peaks that corresponded with political crises or military campaigns. The Russian War Scare was typical. For several months in 1885 the Company was called upon to put right the deterioration of many years of lay-up in reserve that had afflicted the older wooden-hulled ships of the fleet.

The 'Turnabout' principle

The introduction of the Whitehead automobile torpedo in April 1871 intensified interest in this naval weapon, in turn accelerating the development of the torpedo boat and, as a counter-measures response was called for, of the torpedo boat destroyer. Although many of the early torpedo-carrying steam launches had been fitted with tubes, these were of a fixed variety and, because of the size of the craft, aiming them, which depended on craft manoeuvrability, was very difficult. This resulted in the conversion of some launches to carry the original spar torpedo, while in other cases they were fitted with outboard torpedo dropping gear. In these examples aim was achieved by lining up the vessel's head on the target.

White's was concerned that the problem of aiming torpedoes by deck-mounted tubes from steam launches should be overcome, and in 1881 a specially designed 42-foot pinnace was built with two rudders that provided the solution. To create this extremely manoeuvrable vessel, the deadwood aft was reduced to the extent that she could virtually spin around about her centre. This gained her the semi-official name of the 'Turnabout' boat. One balanced rudder was fitted ahead of the propellers so that she steered particularly well when going astern, while the second rudder could be moved to 90 degrees to allow the boat to be virtually stopped dead in the water. Equally, when going ahead, it provided the means of turning the craft through 360 degrees in just 30 seconds.

The Admiralty's normal reaction to such revolutionary design concepts was one of conservatism and restraint, but in this case they recognised immediately the superiority of the 'Turnabout' boat over existing types. Though built by White's speculatively, the Admiralty purchased the special pinnace for service aboard HMS *Inflexible*, then commanded by Captain (later Admiral and First Sea Lord) John Fisher.

Typically, John Samuel White was not content with this creation, despite the praise and adulation emanating from naval circles, and he proceeded to improve the design further. This culminated in a 56-foot steam pinnace incorporating the 'Turnabout' principle, which was so favourably received that it became the pattern for naval steam pinnaces for many years afterwards. Partly in recognition of the achievement of conceiving this highly innovative design, White's became the principal producers of the class, at least one of which was carried by every Royal Navy ship.

With only few modifications, primarily to their form of motive power, 'Turnabout' torpedo pinnaces continued in production for years. Initially, power was supplied by a 156 ihp steam engine weighing 6.5 tons and capable of propelling the vessels at a speed of 15 knots. Later examples were fitted with water-tube boilers, then enclosed forced-lubrication steam engines and, finally, with internal combustion engines.

Torpedo boats - the beginning

True torpedo boats, as distinct from torpedo pinnaces, made their first appearance in 1878 when Torpedo Boat No 19 was constructed, the first of the type to be built by White's for the Royal Navy. It had been around 1870 that John Samuel White had begun seriously to consider developing his high-speed steam launch into a torpedo boat. After the passage of another eight years the opportunity finally arrived to convert these plans to reality.

Torpedo Boat No 19 measured only 87 feet by 11 feet and displaced a mere 28 tons. She carried two small torpedo tubes and was capable of a speed of 21 knots from her 460 ihp engines. Of a very primitive design, her low freeboard and flush deck, which had been stipulated by the Admiralty, made her a poor seaboat. Nevertheless, she was equal to any of her contemporaries built by other shipyards. It remained only for the torpedo boat to be gradually refined, largely through design changes conceived and advocated by White's.

A class of somewhat improved torpedo boats, Nos 34 to 38, were contracted at the time of the Russian War Scare, entering service in 1886-7 and all built on the 'Turnabout' principle. Almost simultaneously a much enlarged torpedo boat, also incorporating the 'Turnabout' principle, was constructed 'on spec' by White's in 1885. HMS *Swift*, later re-identified as HM Torpedo Boat No 81, measured 150 feet in overall length on a displacement tonnage of 125 tons.

The *Swift* was a most interesting vessel in that she represented not only a major advance to the torpedo boat type but also, because White's had designed her with a strengthened stem for ramming other torpedo boats, the prototype of a new class of vessel, the torpedo boat destroyer - this was some eight years before the first true destroyer appeared. As a destroyer she could have mounted three 6-pounder guns with a single 14-inch torpedo tube in her stem, but as a torpedo boat she was completed with six 3-pounder guns and three deck-mounted torpedo tubes.

The *Swift*'s introduction was cleverly arranged, for it occurred at the very time when naval officers were clamouring for more seaworthy torpedo boats with a greater radius of action. In these respects she was conspicuously superior to all other contemporary examples: her freeboard was higher and her overall sea-keeping qualities were a marked improvement; her Belliss-built three-cylinder compound engine driving a single screw was remark-

ably light for its power; her bunkers stowed 35 tons of coal; and in both speed and endurance she excelled. Trials over the measured mile resulted in a mean speed of 20.8 knots, with 22.4 knots the speed achieved on the best of her six runs.

Again, in the *Swift* White's had impressed the Admiralty by its private design, and this led to orders for more torpedo boats. From this point torpedo boat construction for the Royal Navy and foreign navies became a major part of the shipyard's work load. Destroyer construction soon followed, establishing the specialisation with which, by the start of the First World War, White's was automatically associated.

A single Company and modernisation

In 1884 further organisational changes took place which resulted in all of the shipbuilding works, on both sides of the River Medina, coming under the control of John Samuel White, the first time that there had been a single company since 1825, when Joseph White had been allowed to run the Falcon Yard independently of the other shipbuilding operations. John Samuel's two sons, John Lee White and Herbert Samuel White, born in 1862 and 1863 respectively, entered the business at this time to assist their father with the running of the rapidly growing enterprise.

The unification of the Company under a single proprietor provided the opportunity to rationalise the shipyard facilities and resources to better suit the logical stages of the shipbuilding process - not exactly a method of production-line assembly, but the nearest thing to it. In 1884 ships were still being built and launched, engined and fitted out, on both sides of the river, and many operations were being duplicated or, through lack of continuity, were grossly inefficient. John Samuel White determined to remedy all this to make the Company more productive and efficient, improving the turn-around time from keel-laying to delivery and allowing bigger vessels to be built with a competitive price per ton which both naval and commercial customers demanded.

Fundamentally this involved the designation of the Falcon Yard as the location for all future hull construction, with associated activities conveniently sited in support of this. Hence the mould loft, the plate cutting and bending shops, the blacksmiths', anglesmiths' and joiners' shops were all situated in the covered workshops that ran along parallel to Clarence Road, on the landward end of the slipways. Progressively, the remaining building berths on the West Cowes side were closed down and filled in, with the exception of the lifeboat slips and the 200-foot-long launching way that was situated at the northernmost end of the yard.

Extending this philosophy across the river, the Medina Shipyard was to become the Company's fitting-out centre. As the building slips were removed, so the deep water quays would be extended along the river frontage to provide a total length 350 feet for finishing hulls newly launched from East Cowes. Again, all the relevant work-

Right **HM Torpedo Boat No 116 moored in the River Medina.** *White's Archives, Cowes Maritime Museum*

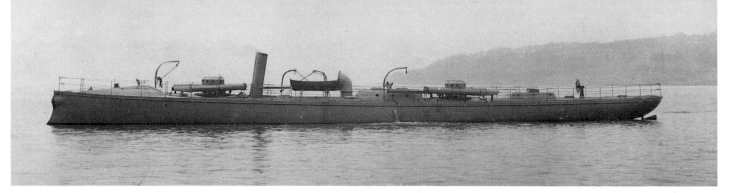

Above The 125-foot 'Turnabout' Torpedo Boat No 34 which was delivered to the Royal Navy in August 1886. She is seen at the entrance to Cowes Harbour. *White's Archives*

Right Torpedo boat development had already progressed significantly when the No 94 to 96 series of boats was commissioned in 1894. The turtle back fo'c'sle is a distinctive feature of these early warships. *White's Archives*

Below HM Torpedo Boat No 95 seen in the River Medina, a view of the local scene dating from the late Victorian era. *White's Archives, Wayne Pritchett collection*

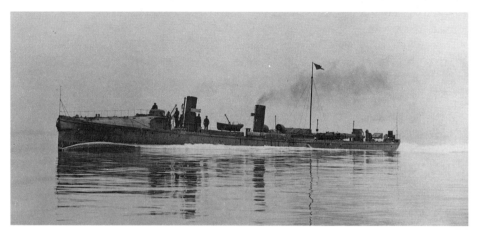

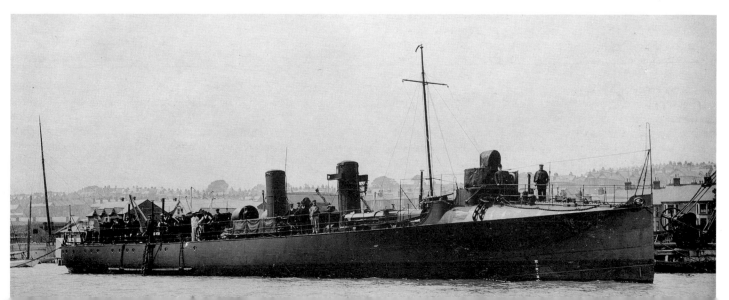

shops and stores were to be placed adjacent to the fitting-out quays, providing a ready supply of all the necessary materials for completing ships.

These were ambitious plans that would take some time to complete, particularly as, beyond the basic scheme to modernise the shipyards in satisfaction of John Samuel's production objectives, a number of new and improved facilities were also proposed. The number of building berths in the Falcon Yard was to be gradually increased to seven, of varying dimensions up to 340 feet, to suit the construction of vessels of a wide range of sizes and types. In support of these, additional cranes would be installed, but, of primary significance, to correct the deficiency that for long had been recognised by John Samuel, the Company was to have its own engineering works and boiler shops.

Engineering Works, West Cowes

George Belliss's company in Birmingham was still making practically all the engines for White's boats, but despite the good working relationship, this was not an ideal arrangement.

It did not suit the policy advocated by John Samuel White who argued that as the shipbuilder's reputation depended on the performance of the whole ship, including its machinery, the responsibility for the fabrication of the *entire* ship should rightly and properly rest with them too. The performance of the engines was critical, of course, for no matter how advanced the hydrodynamic qualities of the hull lines might be, they were as good as useless if the means of propulsion was unreliable or expensive to operate at the designed speed.

In keeping with John Samuel's reorganisation scheme, the new Engineering Works was to be constructed in the West Cowes shipyard, in the area vacated by the clearance of building slips and the surrounding motley collection of small buildings and stores that were scattered about in this vicinity. Further space to provide workshops for non-engineering fitting-out tasks was to be obtained by closing and filling in the drydocks which were now largely redundant anyway. Work commenced in 1889 with the filling in of the old Medina Drydock and the levelling and clearing of the Medina shipyard buildings. By the turn of the century, the bulk of the workshop erection in the West Cowes yard was complete and the Engineering Works was fully operational producing boilers, compound engines for auxiliary yachts and other craft, and a range of other machinery. When the Admiralty opted for turbine propulsion, White's took out a licence to construct Parsons turbines in the Engineering Works.

The opening of the Engineering Works introduced new categories of tradesmen to the White's shipyard range of personnel, among them boilermakers, fitters and specialist engine designers. In this latter respect, the Company was fortunate to secure the services of two outstanding engineers, Andrew Forster, who joined the Company in the early 1890s as Engineering Works Manager, and Edwin Carnt, who went on to become Managing Director. It was in collaboration with Andrew Forster that John Samuel White developed the White water-tube boiler.

The Engineering Department had only been in existence for a few years when a novel coil water-tube boiler, suitable for installation on smaller craft, was invented, designed, built and successfully tested. This consisted primarily of two lower water chambers and an upper steam chest connected by numerous water tubes and enclosed in a casing. Its features included double coils or spirals of small tubes, located around the flues, which were heated by the circulation of the furnace gases. The boiler design was such that the products of combustion had to pass from the grate down the centre of the boiler and then return along the side flues in order to reach the funnel, being brought into contact with the heating surfaces of the coils before losing their heat.

The coil water-tube boiler had a number of clear advantages. Apart from a great saving in weight, it provided a steady supply of steam and was immune from leakages owing to the flexibility of the coils as they expanded. The boiler was particularly accessible for maintenance and cleaning of the heating surfaces. A larger type of water-tube boiler was also constructed and fitted with increasing success. This, too, was progressively improved, culminating in the White-Forster water-tube boiler, patented in 1897. The steam receivers were modified, the water chambers increased to three, all connected together, and the flow of the furnace gases re-directed by a 'water-wall' of straight tubes, all to promote economy of operation by improving combustion and the more efficient absorption of heat by the heating surfaces.

Destroyers

In 1898 the firm became a Private Limited Company, though for the immediate future it remained strictly in the control of the White family and a small number of selected shareholders. The new Company was registered on 11 February 1898.

It was in connection with this change that Mr Edwin Carnt now joined the business. Along with Mr John Lee White, he immediately set about concentrating efforts in pursuing new naval work for the Company, and together they were responsible for the rapid advances in destroyer design and construction which the shipyard made over the next 15 years.

White's continued to build torpedo boats for as long as they were included in the naval building programmes,

Top near right This map of the shipyard in 1898 shows clearly, on the West Cowes side, the expansion of the Engineering Department alongside of Bridge Road (formerly Brunswick Place). The Thetis Dock has disappeared completely and the Medina Drydock has contracted to a very small facility, little bigger than the original Thetis Dock. An interesting feature is the Miniature Rifle Range located in the West Cowes Shipyard. *Isle of Wight Records Office, courtesy Ordnance Survey*

Top far right The Falcon Shipyard, East Cowes, at the same date shows that the yard facilities have expanded significantly by this time with numerous slipways, including a covered slip, and workshops along the length of Clarence Road. Originally the river shore had extended up to the side of Clarence Road. *Isle of Wight Records Office, courtesy Ordnance Survey*

Right White-Forster water-tube boilers for the 'River' Class destroyer HMS *Nith*. *White's Archives, Cowes Maritime Museum*

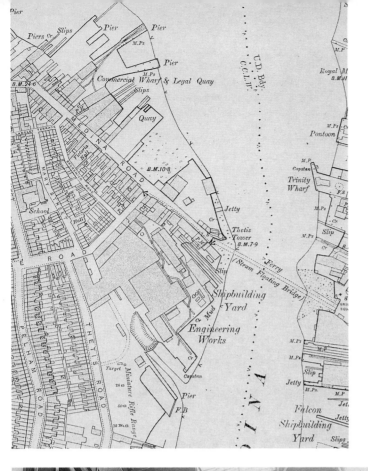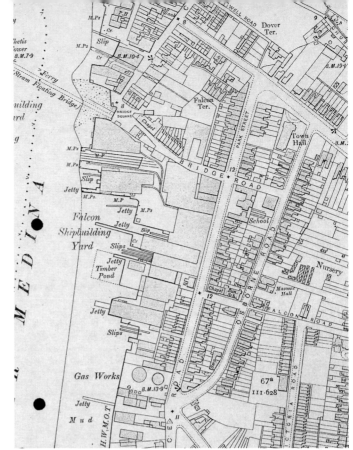

Right Another of the beautiful auxiliary yachts constructed by the Company in this era, the *Zaida* was built for Lord Rosebery in 1900. *White's Archives, Wayne Pritchett collection*

Below The wooden miner *Rodney*, one of a number of similar craft built for the Secretary of State for War around the turn of the century, was delivered in 1902. *White's Archives*

but it was increasingly to the new destroyer classes that the Company's attention was turned as these superseded the earlier class of vessel.

The first experimental torpedo boat destroyers had suggested that this type of ship could make a practical countermeasure to the torpedo boat menace, while at the same time offering a far more suitable platform for launching torpedoes at enemy ships, thereby largely rendering the torpedo boat obsolete except for coastal patrol work. White's was privileged to be among the lead shipyards to be invited by the Admiralty to submit their designs and tender prices for destroyers.

This was a transitional period in the design of warships in that shipyards could still submit their own concepts in response to Admiralty specifications, while the Admiralty also prepared its own designs to which shipyards were invited to construct ships, but with allowance of significant latitude for modifications. Thus shipyards could build to their own designs, to the designs of lead yards which the Admiralty had adopted, or to purely Admiralty designs. White's was no exception to all this and, like other shipbuilders and where permitted, the Company introduced its own alterations and improvements. The result was considerable variation in the performance and appearances of naval vessels, even between ships of the same class.

The first true destroyers built by White's were the three 'A' Class ships ordered in 1894, the *Conflict*, *Teazer* and *Wizard*. These destroyers were conceived by the Admiralty, but White's was given almost unlimited scope to build in its own ideas. They were fitted with Maudslay triple expansion engines providing a speed of 27 knots. Regrettably, one feature insisted on by the Admiralty was a low profile. With inadequate freeboard, they were not good seaboats.

The follow-on requirement of the Navy was for ships of an almost identical design but with the speed increased to 30 knots. John Samuel White considered this design to be understrength for such a power output and would not entertain the contract. This uncompromising attitude denied White's the opportunity for any more destroyer construction for over ten years, but the Company's stance was vindicated when the Armstrong Whitworth-built HMS

Cobra was lost through structural weakness on 17 September 1901 with the loss of 67 lives. Only a month before, on 3 August, the *Cobra*'s sister-ship HMS *Viper*, built by Hawthorn Leslie, had broken in two after running on to rocks off Alderney.

The 1905 programme's specification for 'River' Class destroyers called for much sturdier seaboats, which suited White's philosophy; the Company secured the orders for the *Ness* and *Nith* of this type. Though of an Admiralty design, considerable allowance was granted for builder's modifications. These destroyers were fitted with White's-built coal-fired triple expansion engines, achieving 25.5 knots at 7,250 ihp.

The 'River' Class ships were followed by a series of coastal or sub-destroyers, as they were categorised, constructed in three batches. They featured turtle-back foredecks and a triple screw propulsion arrangement which introduced certain handling difficulties. The engines were oil-fired triple expansion installations producing a speed of 26 knots. The Navy's reversion to oil-firing in these ships, with bunker capacity for up to 24 tons of fuel, led to them being known, unofficially, as the 'Oily Wads'.

The first five were originally named after insects, but subsequently, when they were downgraded to First Class Torpedo Boats, they were rechristened with numbers in keeping with the later-built units. Of a total of 36 ships in the class, 13 were built by White's, minor differences distinguishing the White's batches from each other and from those produced by other yards.

Next the Company built three large, ocean-going destroyers of the 'Tribal' Class, namely the *Mohawk*, *Saracen* and *Crusader*. These ships turned out to be the last British destroyers to be built almost entirely according to White's own designs. They were fitted with White's-built oil-fired steam turbines connected with White-Forster boilers, a particularly effective combination. Against a contract speed of 33 knots, the *Mohawk* logged a trial speed of 34.3 knots. The other two performed

HMS *Teazer*, one of the three 'A' Class destroyers built by White's, was launched on 9 February 1895. She is seen here alongside the fitting-out quay at West Cowes. *White's Archives, Cowes Maritime Museum*

equally well and, at one point, the *Crusader* was one of the fastest destroyers in the fleet.

In the 1908 programme, White's received orders for the *Basilisk* and *Harpy* of the *'Beagle'* Class. In the 1909 programme they were awarded contracts for the *Redpole*, *Rifleman* and *Ruby* of the *'Acorn'* Class. To these were added the improved *Ferret* and *Forrester*, ordered under the 1910 estimates. All these destroyers were built to the standardised designs of the Admiralty's Director of Naval Construction, with virtually no scope for builder-conceived alterations. Nevertheless, they were all excellent ships that performed well, and which in most cases exceeded their contracted specifications.

In 1912 White's secured an order from the Chilean Navy to construct six super-destroyers or flotilla leaders; with the exception of HMS *Swift*, built in 1907, they were the biggest destroyers in the world at that time. From the Company's point of view these ships represented the perfect opportunity to demonstrate once again their total design and build capability for warships of this type, something which the imposition of Admiralty standard designs had denied them as far as British vessels were concerned.

The Chilean flotilla leaders were remarkable vessels in every way because, without sacrificing the high speed and other features typical of first-rate destroyers, they also had to fulfil the functions of cruisers, patrolling Chile's long coastline. With dimensions of 320 feet by 32.5 feet and a full load displacement of 1,850 tons, their 27,000 shp turbine engines gave them a speed of 31 knots. Armament consisted of six 4-inch guns, two machine guns and three 18-inch torpedo tubes. Four of the Class that were still under construction when the war started were commandeered by the Royal Navy for war service. So well did they perform that, when the war was over and Chile was offered compensation, the war-worn veterans were taken back in preference to the option of new ships.

The final group of pre-First World War destroyers built by White's were the *Laurel*, *Liberty* and the larger *Lightfoot*, which was completed as a flotilla leader to a design influenced by the Chilean super-destroyers.

The demand for destroyers had increased so rapidly that it became necessary to extend the fitting out accommodation. Accordingly, between 1911 and 1912 land was reclaimed along the West Cowes river frontage and the remaining drydocks were filled in. The result was a 350-foot-long straight quay alongside which the large 80-ton hammerhead crane, already referred to, was erected. With existing quays, the total quay frontage for fitting-out purposes was now approximately 600 feet in length.

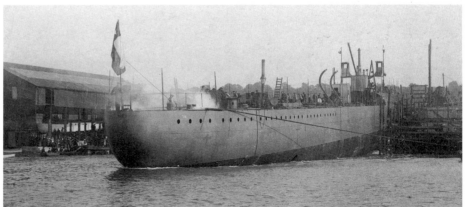

Left The 'Tribal' Class destroyer *Saracen* following her launch on 31 March 1908.

Below left Launch of the repeat 'Acorn' Class destroyer *Ferrett* on 12 April 1911. The picture conveys very well just how labour-intensive shipbuilding was in those days.

Above An important workshop in the Engineering Department was the boiler shop, where the Company's famous White-Forster water-tube boilers were manufactured. The picture shows boilers in various stages of construction, destined for the destroyers *Almirante Lynch* and *Almirante Condell*, yard numbers 1362 and 1363.

Above right Launch of the Chilean flotilla leader *Tome*, later renamed *Almirante Lynch*, on 28 September 1912. She was delivered in 1914.

Right Lowering the White-Forster water-tube boilers aboard the *Almirante Lynch*. The *Almirante Lynch* and *Almirante Condell* were re-armed and modernised by White's in the 1930s. *All photographs White's Archives, Cowes Maritime Museum*

Aircraft Department

A further example of White's inclination to technological adaptation and innovation came on 1 January 1913 with the official opening of the J. Samuel White & Company Aircraft Department. Progress in the development of aircraft from the first primitive flying machines had reached the point where White's, having recognised the future potential of this mode of transport, determined that they should diversify into this line of business.

At that time the Solent region was fast becoming the home of the infant British aircraft industry. On the island, the S.E. Saunders Limited boatyard in East Cowes was already collaborating with the Sopwith Aviation Company Limited in the production of early amphibious aeroplanes. (Saunders went on to form the flying boat constructors Saunders-Roe after the famous aviator, Alliott Verdon Roe, joined them in the 1920s). On the Hampshire side of the Solent, on the Hamble River, Luke & Company had been formed in 1912, later becoming the nucleus of the Admiralty's Marine Aircraft Acceptance Depot. The Hampshire Aero Club had only recently been formed and a new Naval Air Station was established at Calshot in March 1913 for the Naval Wing of the Royal Flying Corps. Many of the early aircraft competitions also took place over the sheltered waters of the Solent, for the most part involving waterborne floatplanes which were being developed with naval patrol applications in mind. All this suggested that this new line of manufacture was not so far removed from White's traditional business as may first have seemed the case.

In keeping with the Company's established practice of embarking on all new undertakings in a thoroughly professional and businesslike manner, the highly respected pioneer British aircraft designer, Howard T. Wright, was engaged and appointed as General Manager and Chief Designer of the Aircraft Department. A succession of increasingly effective floatplane-type aircraft was produced under the tradename of 'The Wight Navyplane' (a name that owed something to each of White, Wright and Isle of Wight) with, right from the start, the Royal Navy targeted as the principal customer. The first two 'Wight' seaplanes to be commissioned by the Royal Naval Air Service satisfactorily passed their acceptance tests in April 1914. During the First World War, the Company's output of aircraft was a major contribution to the national war effort.

The outbreak of the Great War in August 1914 heralded dramatic and far-reaching changes to the political order of Europe and, eventually, the world as a whole. It more or less coincided with another important turn of events in the history of the White shipbuilding company. In spite of failing health, which for some time had prevented him from playing, as he desired, a full part in the daily affairs of the business, John Samuel White was still serving as Company Chairman at 76 years of age. In May 1915 he died at his home at Fishbourne, Isle of Wight. To the very end he continued to take an interest in all that was going on at the shipyard.

Following the First World War, in 1919, just four years after John Samuel's death, his sons sold their shares in the Company to Cardiff-based business interests, thereby terminating the direct link between the White family and the shipbuilding firm. However, the shipyard was to continue under the illustrious name of their father until virtually the end of its existence. In 1914, over 75 per cent of the trade and commerce of the Port of Cowes depended on the J. Samuel White & Company shipyard.

Left and above right **Turbine construction in the long 'A' Shop or Heavy Machine Shop, seen in 1908, part of the Engineering Department complex in the West Cowes Shipyard. The date indicates how early White's began manufacturing steam turbine engines under licence.**
White's Archives, Cowes Maritime Museum

Right Firemen sifting through the severely damaged remains of part of the
Engineering Workshops in West Cowes
following a disastrous fire in November
1912. *Photographer unknown*

3. FIRST WORLD WAR PRODUCTION

In both World Wars, the J. Samuel White Company achieved a magnificent productive output to support the nation's efforts on the battle fronts of the conflict. The firm was particularly highly complimented by the Admiralty, in a special letter of appreciation from the Lords Commissioners, for the rapidity with which the 'P' and 'PC' patrol vessels were built, engined and equipped. During the First World War, the Company's output comprised both warships and naval aircraft, as follows. The dates quoted are delivery dates.

Destroyers (total 27)

Faulknor (ex-*Almirante Simpson*)	24 August 1914
Broke (ex-*Almirante Goni*)	3 November 1914
Botha (ex-*Almirante Williams Robelledo*)	30 March 1915
Tipperary (ex-*Almirante Riveros*)	2 June 1915
Lightfoot	25 September 1914
Magic (ex-*Marigold*)	8 January 1916
Moresby (ex-*Marlion*)	7 April 1916
Medina (ex-*Redmill*)	30 June 1916
Medway (ex-*Redwing*)	2 August 1916
Sable	30 November 1916
Setter	12 February 1917
Trenchant	30 April 1917
Tristram	30 June 1917
Vampire	22 September 1917
Vectis	5 December 1917
Vortigern	25 January 1918
Winchelsea	15 March 1918
Winchester	29 April 1918
Tribune	16 July 1918
Trinidad	9 September 1918
Trojan	6 December 1918
Truant	17 March 1919
*Trusty**	9 May 1919
*Witherington**	
*Wivern**	all completed
*Wolverine**	in 1920
*Worcester**	

* ships launched after the Armistice

Patrol Vessels (total 11)

P11	27 January 1916
P12	26 February 1916
P40	31 October 1916
P52	22 December 1916
P59	27 February 1917
PC67 (Q-ship)	29 June 1917
PC68 (Q-ship)	3 August 1917
PC71 (Q-ship)	7 May 1918
PC72 (Q-ship)	1 October 1918
PC73 (Q-ship)	31 October 1918
PC74 (Q-ship)	23 December 1918

Submarines (total 2)

E32	24 October 1916
F2	27 August 1917

The order for submarine *G15*, placed in 1915, was cancelled.

Miscellaneous small craft (total *circa* 60)

Seaplanes (total 201)

Wight Improved Navyplane - 11 machines
Admiralty Type 840 Seaplane - 30 machines
Wight Converted Seaplane - 40 machines
Short 184 Seaplane - 101 machines
Miscellaneous aircraft - 19 machines

White's total First World War production:
100 ships
201 aircraft

Besides this the Company undertook numerous overhaul, refit and repair tasks.

Throughout the war, White's-built ships, both of pre-war and wartime construction, performed yeoman service with the Royal Navy. Inevitably, though, there were losses, the major warship casualties being HMS *Tipperary* sunk by gunfire at the Battle of Jutland on 31 May 1916 with the loss of 185 lives, the HMS *P12* sunk in the English Channel, also in 1916, and HMS *Setter* which was lost in collision with the destroyer HMS *Sylph* in thick fog off Harwich on 17 May 1917.

At the outbreak of the Great War, J. Samuel White & Company had a total of eight building berths, the largest big enough to take vessels of up to 340 feet in length. There also was a 350-foot patent hauling-up slipway which was capable of raising a ship with a displacement of 600 tons.

In spite of the Company's pre-occupation with war construction, improvements to the yard's facilities continued apace. Building berths numbers 2 and 4 were reconstructed in concrete, new steel building sheds were erected with overhead electrical travelling cranes, and a new timber store was constructed in the Clarence Yard at the southern end of the Falcon Yard, East Cowes. To satisfy the demanding wartime production quotas, the yards were equipped with large amounts of new machinery of all kinds, including a new electrical jib crane located at the end of the North Pier.

Right **The shipyards' layout as it was in 1914, at the outbreak of the First World War. The development of the Engineering Department at West Cowes has continued, while the remains of the Medina Drydock have by this time disappeared altogether.** *Isle of Wight Records Office, courtesy of Ordnance Survey*

Left HMS *Broke* (ex-*Almirante Goni*), seen here on trials, earned special distinctions for one of the most courageous actions performed by any of His Majesty's ships during the First World War. On 20 April 1917, while attached to the Dover patrol under the command of Captain E. Evans, she encountered and attacked six enemy warships. The first German destroyer, *G42*, was rammed and heavily damaged by shellfire, the second, *G85*, was torpedoed and sunk, while the third was rammed amidships. The two ships remained locked together, so the order was given aboard the *Broke* to draw cutlasses, and fierce hand-to-hand fighting ensued. After disengaging from her sinking adversary, the *Broke* managed to fire two torpedoes, sinking the fourth enemy ship, even though, by this time, she was herself severely damaged by shellfire. The *Broke*'s performance is all the more remarkable when the armaments of the vessels on either side are compared. The *Broke* and a companion ship had between them only one 6-inch gun and eight 4-inch guns. The German destroyers, in contrast, mounted in total 18 4-inch guns, while their combined torpedo tubes exceeded by 30 those available to the British ships. *White's Archives*

Below HMS *Sable*, an 'R' Class Emergency War destroyer launched on 26 June 1916 (nearest the camera), alongside the fitting-out quays at West Cowes. The White Ensign at her stern suggests that she is visiting the J. Samuel White shipyard for a refit. The two ships, ahead of her and on her inside, appear to be two of the later 'S' Class destroyers. On 13 April 1918, during a steam trial, the *Sable* achieved a maximum speed of 35.2 knots. Later she provided escort assistance to the surrendering German Battle Fleet. *White's Archives*

Left White's built only two submarines during the First World War, the *E32* and *F2*, and one of them is seen here under construction in the covered slipway in East Cowes, demolished during the early 1920s, that lay alongside what came to be known as the Submarine Shed. The so-called Submarine Shed, which was located at the northern end of the Falcon Yard and in which, quite probably, no submarines were actually built, continued to bear this identity until its demolition in the 1970s. *White's Archives, Cowes Maritime Museum*

Below The *P11* was one of a particularly distinctive type of patrol vessel or submarine destroyer for which White's was complimented by the Admiralty in recognition of the speed with which they were completed. These vessels were given a very distinctive shape, which was intended to resemble a submarine, so as to deceive U-boats and lure them into the range of the patrol vessels' superior firepower. *Imperial War Museum*

Bottom left Another, quite different, type of patrol vessel, the *PC67*. This vessel and her sisters were 'Q ships', or decoy vessels. They were fast and heavily armed, their purpose being to draw U-boats on to apparently defenceless merchantmen where they would be overwhelmed by rapid shellfire. In practice, Q ships were not as successful as had been hoped. *White's Archives, Cowes Maritime Museum*

Right J. Samuel White & Company's other major contribution to the war effort during the First World War was in the form of aircraft production, an activity that had been started in 1913. Shown here on the water, after launching from the Gridiron Yard at East Cowes, is one of the early Wight Navyplanes. When aircraft production got under way in quantity, the Gridiron Yard was disposed of and manufacturing transferred across the river to West Cowes. The picture caption advises that the aircraft depicted was launched for the first time on 5 May 1913 and was lost in a crash on 13 May! *Photographer unknown*

Right A Wight Converted Seaplane in the River Medina alongside the slipway in the West Cowes shipyard. Prior to the opening of the Somerton Works, the majority of the floatplane construction took place in the West Cowes shipyard. *White's Archives*

Below A Shorts 184 floatplane on the slipway at West Cowes. Although not a White's aircraft design, this was a type that the Company built in greater numbers than any other. *Science Museum*

4. VOLUME AND VARIETY

The return of peace in 1919 resulted in a sudden deceleration in all warship construction and other manufacturing work producing armaments. Thus the last four modified 'W' Class destroyers on the order book were cancelled, the *Westphal* (yard no 1542) and *Westward Ho* (yard no 1543) in December 1918, and the *Wrangler* (yard no 1528) and *Werewolf* (yard no 1541) in September 1919, the incomplete hulls of the latter pair having to be dismantled. This downturn in naval construction that followed the war was initially offset, after a two-year lull, by a glut of merchant orders to make good the heavy losses of commercial shipping through the war years. But the next 20 years was a difficult period in which White's had to come to terms with the near absence of warship orders, other than those they could secure from foreign navies.

The Company made this adjustment most successfully so that, in spite of the recession of the early 1920s and the far more damaging effects of the Great Depression throughout the 1930s, White's still accomplished a quite prodigious volume of construction of immense variety of size and type, a total of 345 vessels, including 84 lifeboats for the RNLI and numerous other smaller craft and boats. The superior vessel types comprised, on the mercantile side, ten cargo ships of various types, six large steel colliers, three oil barges, a lightship, five paddle ferries, two paddle steamers, two steamers for the Great Lakes, and five large private yachts, either sail, steam or motor. Naval construction, which increased as rearmament resumed in earnest in the 1930s, was made up of 18 destroyers, four sloops, a river gunboat, a large patrol vessel and two large harbour vessels.

Compared with any preceding peacetime period of 20 years, this proved to be the most productive era to date in the Company's history, in terms of new tonnage built. Even so, the output of larger vessel types was still somewhat below the shipyard's increased capacity, a sign of the very difficult times for the shipbuilding industry in general throughout these years.

On the aircraft side it proved to be much less easy to adapt from military to civil aircraft construction, particularly as there was a huge surplus of warplanes which were being converted for fare-paying passenger-carrying operations. Towards the end of the First World War, the Aircraft Department had been primarily engaged in manufacturing seaplanes to the designs of the Shorts Aircraft Company of Rochester, Kent, and propellers for Handley Page. There were no new White's designs in the pipeline, nor were there likely to be.

No doubt perceiving the inevitable closure of the Company's aircraft business, Howard Wright resigned from White's Aircraft Department in September 1917 to pursue his profession in his own consultancy firm. He was replaced by Mr T. C. Letcher as Chief Designer, and Wing Commander Gerald Aldwell as General Manager.

In November 1918, with the cessation of hostilities, even the orders for Short 184s was cut back. The appointment of a new board of directors in the same month heralded a return to the Company's traditional work for which it was world-renowned and on which it now intended to concentrate its efforts. Certainly there was no profit to be made from aircraft construction for the foreseeable future.

The Aircraft Department was officially closed on 28 July 1919, all production work having ceased the previous January. Between then and the mid-1920s White's strove without success to dispose of the Cowes Aerodrome, the hangars and the Somerton Workshops. The asking price was £5,000 for the aerodrome and £40,000 for Somerton Works. For some time there were genuine hopes that the aerodrome could become an RAF Training Station and dedicated Repair Depot, which, of course, would have ensured some continuity of employment at a time when jobs in the local economy were declining. This was not to be, however, for, as the Air Ministry pointed out, there was an abundance of similar facilities at their disposal all around the country.

In April 1919 the Avro Aircraft Company expressed interest in the hangars at the aerodrome, but this sale did not materialise either. Eventually the airfield was leased to Saunders-Roe as a test centre for their A10 fighters, Spartan landplanes and licence-built Blackburn Bluebird Mk 4 biplanes. Later, up to the Second World War, scheduled air services were operated between the aerodrome and London's Heston and Croydon airports.

Similarly, the Somerton Works could not be disposed of readily. After remaining empty for some time it was used for the manufacture of motor buses, then motor scooters and, lastly, for the production of the final batch of Spartan Cruisers, while Saunders-Roe's new Columbine Works at East Cowes was being completed. The Somerton Works remained in the ownership of J. Samuel White & Company, which proved beneficial after the Second World War, permitting the resumption of engineering work in association with the continuing shipbuilding programme at Cowes.

The remaining aircraft construction and assembly sheds at West Cowes reverted in 1919 to engineering work and small boat building.

After having been a private concern for 21 years, the firm was finally made into a public limited company in 1919, completing the administrative reconstruction that had been planned at the time of John Samuel White's death but which the intervening war had prevented.

The momentum of the postwar commercial shipbuilding programme got under way with a string of orders for steel colliers for British and foreign owners, the *Argonne* and *Auvergne* for the Compania Delmas of France, the *Bilton*, *River Wear* and *River Tees* for Lythgoe Prince Ship Management, and the *Atlas* for the Norwegian shippers A/S Atlas (Jacobson & Co).

These were followed by a quantity of orders for cargo

Simplified location map showing the geographical disposition of the principal manufacturing and experimental sites at Cowes, Isle of Wight, occupied by J. Samuel White & Company.
1: East Cowes Shipyard, c1803-1965
2: West Cowes Shipyard, c1820-1981
3: Thetis Dock and Shipyard, 1815-c1912
4: Cowes Areodrome, c1916-c1939
5: Somerton Works, 1917-1969
6: Gridiron Yard, East Cowes, c?-c1915
7: Henry Bannisters Ropeworks, 1956-1968
D. L. Williams, based on original material

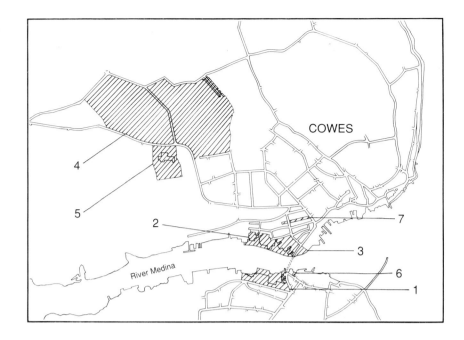

Fitting out of the 265-foot steel cargo steamer *Hitherwood*, yard number 1562, launched on 1 July 1922. *White's Archives, Cowes Maritime Museum*

ships, all fulfilled between 1920 and 1922. First came orders for two new ships, followed by two more for repairs to the Norwegian vessels *Svane* and *Evanger*. Two additional new construction contracts completed the group. The largest of the four new ships was the 256-foot-long *Hitherwood*, built for C. A. Stewart. Orders for three more cargo ships for Puissesseau Cie were unfortunately cancelled.

This left an unwelcome gap in the order book and the mainstay of the shipyard's work for the foreseeable future was lifeboat building for the RNLI. Between 1923 and 1939 White's built a total of 84 new craft for the Institution, an unrivalled volume of deliveries in the interwar period.

In 1922 the Company established a subsidiary, the Island Transport Company, fundamentally a coastal cargo shipping and road haulage operation. This was run, first and foremost, as a commercial service between Cowes and Southampton, but it was also set up for strategic reasons. Being island-based and receiving many of its materials and components from suppliers on the mainland of Great Britain, the Company was constantly burdened with high shipping costs which threatened to make shipyard prices less competitive. Not only did this Company-run service reduce cross-Solent transportation costs to the minimum, but the commercial trade that it handled further subsidised the carriage of shipyard-bound supplies.

From around the mid-1920s the Island Transport Company proved to be equally beneficial for the carriage of White's traffic going in the other direction. Having abandoned all the dry docks at Cowes, White's had only limited means for offering a repair and overhaul service for ships turning round at Southampton. It was decided by the Company that, in view of the large amount of work which had to be done on ships docking at Southampton, it would be advantageous to have a complete repair plant centrally situated within Southampton

Docks. Consequently extensive workshops were erected close to the Prince of Wales Drydock, on the River Itchen side of the Old Docks complex. These facilities were laid out and equipped to deal with all kinds of repair and overhaul work. The various departments included a hull repair section, supported by a blacksmiths' shop, a coppersmiths' shop and a large joiners' and pattern-makers' shop, and an engine fitting and machine shop. All the larger shops were equipped with overhead electrical cranes.

The Southampton Repair Department was valuable to White's in another way, taking on in the drydock the removal of launch cradles and the cleaning and painting of the hulls of new vessels built on the Island prior to the commencement of their trials.

The Island Transport Company maintained the link between the Repair Department at Southampton and the main White's shipyard at Cowes with a fleet of small motor barges and lighters. Over the period from 1923 to 1974 seven vessels in total were owned and operated for varying durations by the Island Transport Company.

Repair and refit work continued to be an important part of the Company's work at Cowes too, particularly at times when orders for new ships were only being received erratically. Much of this involved the conversion of surplus naval tonnage for civilian roles. For instance, a group of eight double-ended gunboats were rebuilt as cargo vessels. Some of these were gutted internally in order to provide adequate cargo holds, while others were lengthened and subjected to other modifications as appropriate to the new work for which they would be employed. All in all, by the time they left the shipyard on the completion of the renovation, they were unrecognisable from their original appearance.

Other conversion work undertaken was intended to give a new lease of life to naval craft exhausted from long years of intensive war duties. Laid up idle with vast quan-

The *Panther*, one of the four Greek destroyers refitted by White's in 1924. As originally built these ships had five funnels - combining the boiler flue trunkings into two funnels, as shown here, resulted in a very distinctive, though unattractive, profile. *White's Archives*

Right The launch of the famous Thames 'Butterfly Boat' excursion steamer *Crested Eagle*, yard Number 1621, on 26 March 1920. *White's Archives, Cowes Maritime Museum*

Below The completed *Crested Eagle* on trials, clearly showing her telescopic funnel which could be retracted to provide clearance under London Bridge. *White's Archives, Cowes Maritime Museum*

tities of other war surplus material, these vessels were eminently sellable, offering a valuable opportunity to derive income to help restore the national economy that was ailing from the massive military expenditure imposed by the war. White's contribution to this effort took the form of converting eight former minesweepers into armed patrol vessels for the Spanish Government.

One of the most interesting jobs of this kind, taken on in 1924, which allowed White's to apply the accumulated experience of its many years of specialist naval work, was the complete refurbishment and engine overhaul of four Greek destroyers, the *Ierax*, *Leon*, *Aetos* and *Panther*. The work on these prewar four-funnelled warships included a thorough reconditioning of all engine, accommodation and control spaces, re-boilering with White-Forster water-tube boilers and rearming. They left the shipyard, substantially altered in appearance, with fighting power, propelling machinery and speed more befitting modern warships of that period.

This was no more or less than had been specified, but in one aspect it deserves special mention as a consequence to a story that commenced with the building of

these ships. Ordered originally from Cammell Laird by the Argentine Government as part of a sizeable order for large and fast destroyers placed on British, German and French shipyards, their ambitious specification called for, among other things, a top speed of 35 knots. Unlike their foreign-built consorts, though, these four ships just failed to meet their contract speed on trials and, hence, were rejected by the Argentines. The problem of how to dispose of them was resolved by selling them to the Greeks to strengthen their navy for the war with Turkey in which they were then engaged. Interestingly, as a result of White's refurbishment, their maximum speed was increased to 2 knots better than the trial speed that had been stipulated in the original building contract. The successful completion of this work assisted the Company in securing additional naval orders from foreign governments in the years that followed.

Between 1922 and 1930, White's took on the building of a series of passenger-carrying craft. First the yard commenced the construction of two of what eventually turned out to be a quartet of paddle ferries for the London County Council for the Woolwich Ferry cross-Thames

One of the two chain ferries or floating bridges delivered by White's in 1925, the Poole Ferry No 1. *White's Archives, Cowes Maritime Museum*

passenger and vehicle service. These were the *Squires* completed in 1922, and the *Gordon*, delivered the following year. These ferries were of the flush-deck type with accommodation on two decks, 100 passengers on the main deck and 90 tons of vehicles on a large amidships deck structure. A second pair of almost identical ferries of this type, the *John Benn* and *Will Crook*, were built in 1930.

In 1924, when the General Steam Navigation Company Limited decided to add a modern paddle steamer to its fleet of vessels operating excursion services between London and coastal resorts on the Thames and the Isle of Thanet, White's submitted a tender which was accepted and which resulted in the *Crested Eagle*. As one of the most attractive vessels to operate on the Thames 'Butterfly Boats' cruises, the *Crested Eagle* was the product of White's extensive experience in the design of shallow draught vessels. She was 309 feet long, almost 70 feet in beam over her paddle sponsons, and could carry 1,700 passengers at a speed of 18.75 knots. Her triple expansion diagonal engines were oil-fired and she was fitted with a telescopic funnel and hinged mast to permit her to pass under London Bridge.

On the outbreak of the Second World War the *Crested Eagle* was commissioned for minesweeping duties. In 1940 she was directed to the French Coast to assist the evacuation of the British Expeditionary Force from the Dunkerque beaches. During the operation, on 29 May, she was attacked and bombed by German aircraft. Set alight and blazing from end to end, she ran ashore and sank. Over 300 of her complement, crew members and troops, were lost in the disaster.

Following on from the *Crested Eagle*, as something of an unusual diversion, came contracts to build two chain ferries. The first of these, Floating Bridge No 2, was for the service across the River Medina between West and East Cowes, immediately alongside the shipyard. The

other was for the Bournemouth & Swanage Company, to maintain the link between Sandbanks and Studland Bay at the entrance to Poole Harbour. These peculiarly shaped craft, out of keeping with the normal, sea-kindly products that the yard was more used to producing, presented certain technical difficulties in their construction and launching, none of which, however, prevented their completion and delivery to date and to price. Indeed, White's followed up these vessels with a third craft of the same type in 1936, the diesel-electric Floating Bridge No 3, again for operation on the passenger and vehicle service between the two parts of Cowes.

The Southern Railway Company was the customer for the other paddle steamer built in this period. This was the attractive little *Freshwater*, completed in 1927 for the cross-Solent services from Lymington to Yarmouth. She served her owners and their successors in the era of nationalisation of the railways up to 1960 when she was sold to new owners; as the *Swanage Queen* she was finally paid off for scrap in May 1962. Although only 264 gross tons and 160 feet long she had excellent accommodation and, being able to achieve a speed of 12 knots, she could comfortably make the Solent crossing in the scheduled 30 minutes.

In all these endeavours, tackling all manner of challenges that confronted the Company, White's exhibited the enterprise that had first established its reputation in the 19th century. As a further example of the diversity of vessel types built by White's in these years, the Great Lakes steamers *Judge Hart* and *Norman P. Clement*, delivered in 1923 for the Eastern Steamship Company, satisfied a typically difficult specification. Measuring 252 feet in overall length, they featured a style traditional to vessels operated on the Great Lakes of engines aft with the main superstructure at the stern and the bridge structure placed well forward over the bows. The amidships cargo holds separated the two structures.

White's long association with the Crown Agents for the Colonies, the India Office and the various Harbour Trusts, Police, Customs and Pilotage Authorities continued to generate a steady flow of orders for multi-tasked small

Right The third *Xarifa* (yard number 1686) built for F. Mortimer Singer was a steam yacht. She was 178 feet long and had a maeirform bow. *White's Archives, Cowes Maritime Museum*

Below The Falcon Shipyard, East Cowes, in the late 1920s, showing, among other features, the slipways, Joiners' Shop, Platers' Shop and Mould Loft above the Boat Shop. The Engineer

Bottom The West Cowes Shipyard at the same date, being a detailed plan of the workshops and fitting-out facilities. The Engineer

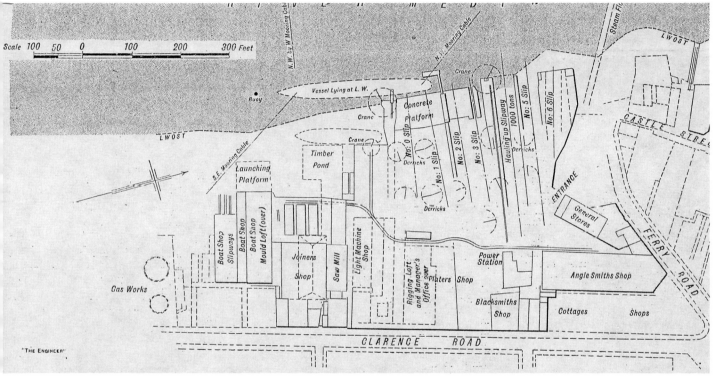

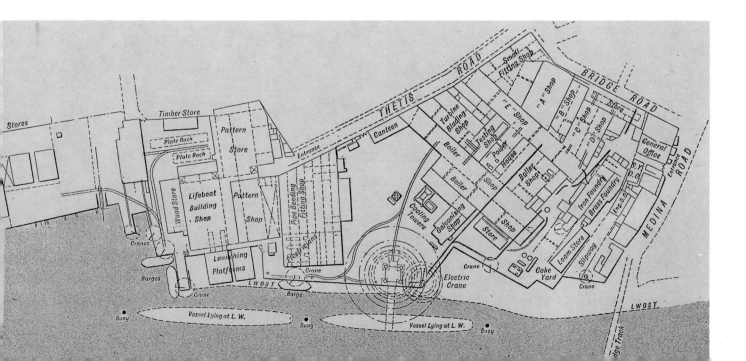

craft for harbour and coastal duties. Yacht construction, too, remained a constant and dependable source of new work. Mr F. M. Singer, the New York owner of the Singer Sewing Machine Company, who had commissioned the beautiful 193-foot, 363-ton auxiliary steam yacht *Xarifa* back in 1894, came back to the Company for two more private yachts, each christened with the same name. The second *Xarifa*, another auxiliary vessel, delivered in 1927, was sold on to a new owner soon after, to be followed by the third vessel of the name, a 178-foot steam yacht built in 1930. This latter craft is believed to be still afloat.

The needs of the shipping industry were constantly changing; in order to keep pace the technology of shipbuilding was also subject to a continuous process of evolution. Thus White's, in parallel with competitive shipyards, was always mindful of the need to improve and upgrade the yards' facilities. By 1930 this rolling programme of modernisation had resulted in further readily discernible alterations to the buildings, slipways and other amenities.

The building berths, now reduced to six, nevertheless

included a covered slipway, reducing interference of the building programme by the weather, a feature that was more akin to the kind of facility provided in modern ship-building yards. The patent slip was now capable of hauling up vessels of up to 1,800 tons, increasing the yard's scope for repair work. At the same time the capacity of the Boatbuilding Department had been increased to allow 12 of the largest type of lifeboats to be constructed simultaneously. Further haul-up slips were also provided in this area so that machinery could be installed prior to re-launch.

In the workshops the size of the mould loft, at that time located above the main Boatbuilding Shop in East Cowes, was large enough for a destroyer class of ship to be laid out full size. By contrast, Thornycrofts at Southampton, a long-time rival of White's, could only lay out ships at 1:10 scale.

By this time the Company's main offices had been relocated in West Cowes in a new building erected in Medina Road, on the northern boundary of the shipyard estate. The drawing offices were also located in this area, between the Engineering Shops and the Main Office.

Although the emphasis during the 1920s and 1930s was on the construction of commercial craft, military ships continued to be built, the shipyard reinforcing its reputation for high-speed, high-performance destroyers in two foreign orders and a number of useful warships built for the Royal Navy in the run-up to the Second World War.

The Argentine Government's order for flotilla leaders produced three striking ships, the *Mendoza*, *La Rioja* and *Tucuman*. These vessels were impressive by any standard.

The role of the destroyer had continued to evolve, its three principal categories having been determined soon after the turn of the century when the torpedo boat destroyer, as it had been originally conceived, emerged into the modern warship that played such a vital role in both World Wars. These categories were, in effect, the developed torpedo boat, a small craft of limited range employed increasingly as a coastal patrol vessel, the large or super destroyer-type which satisfied the need for a more powerful vessel to lead groups of destroyers, the so-called flotilla leaders, and, finally, the true destroyer which served primarily as an anti-submarine escort. The three Argentine ships fell in the super-destroyer category and they deserved this description for more reasons than just their size.

Displacing 1,570 tons, they measured 332 feet in overall length. Their most important and most impressive vital statistic was their top speed, contracted at 38 knots and more than achieved by all three on their official trials. *La Rioja*, the third of the trio, created what was claimed at the time to be a world record for a vessel of this class, by her achievement of a speed of 39.4 knots.

Two years after the Argentine ships had been delivered, HMS *Kempenfelt*, a 'Crusader' Class flotilla leader, was built for the Royal Navy. After two more years, the very similarly sized destroyers *Forester* and *Fury* of the 'Fearless' Class were completed. Between then and 1936, when the next British destroyer order was received, the follow-on orders for Royal Navy ships were for the 'Halcyon' Class sloops *Niger* and *Salamander*.

In 1935 White's was awarded the orders for the two destroyers for which, above all others, they are justifiably most famous and which, due to the wartime exploits of one of the pair, have a particularly special association with the town of Cowes. These were the 3,380 tons full load displacement Polish destroyers *Grom* and *Blyskawica*, names which translate into English as the 'Thunder' and 'Lightning'. The contracts were secured against the keenest competition, bids having been submitted by virtually every specialist destroyer shipbuilder from every established shipbuilding country in the world. The end result, designed, built and engined totally by J. Samuel White & Company, more than vindicated the Polish Government's selection of builder. The *Grom* and *Blyskawica* surpassed their contract specification in every way; besides which, they were visually stylish, particularly impressive at speed, and excellent seaboats. At a length of 377 feet, they were the longest ships built by White's up to that time. Their maximum speed was similar to that of the Argentine flotilla leaders. Armament comprised

The launch of the 'Crusader' Class destroyer Kempenfelt on 29 October 1931. *White's Archives, Cowes Maritime Museum*

Left Assembling the keel blocks in readiness for the laying of the keel for the 'Fearless' Class destroyer *Forester*, the second White's ship of that name. *White's Archives, Cowes Maritime Museum*

Right The *Forester* enters the water on 28 June 1934. The *Fury*, on the slipway to the right, will follow in just under three months. *White's Archives, Cowes Maritime Museum*

Left The *Forester* and *Fury* alongside each other fitting out at West Cowes. *White's Archives, Cowes Maritime Museum*

The flag bearing the 'W' at her stern indicates that HMS *Fury* is in the process of undergoing builder's trials. The *Fury* sank after hitting a mine off the coast of France on 21 June 1944, while supporting the Normandy landings. *White's Archives*

The second 'Halcyon' Class sloop, *Salamander*, was launched on 24 March 1936. In the background the Polish destroyers *Grom* and *Blyskawica* are taking shape. *White's Archives*

seven 120 mm main guns and six 550 mm torpedo tubes.

After the outbreak of the Second World War and the defeat of Poland, the *Grom* and *Blyskawica*, then operating with the Free Polish Forces, were attached to and served with the ships of the Royal Navy. In the spring of 1942 the *Blyskawica* was at the White's shipyard at Cowes for a refit. At this time the town and the shipyard began to come under attack from German air raids.

During the night of 4 May 1942 there was a particularly concerted attempt by the German aircraft to inflict serious and widespread damage. It was on this same night that the *Blyskawica* was instrumental in saving a large part of Cowes from being destroyed. Due to the Government directive that all ships should retain their ammunition when in port (a practice not allowed in peacetime), she was fully armed. The raid was a very heavy one, with over 200 tons of high explosive and incendiary bombs being dropped on the area, but the crew of the *Blyskawica* fought tirelessly all that night, her guns

becoming so hot that cold water was constantly being played on them to cool them down.

Dawn found the gun crews still at their posts. It also found someone else at his post. Nightshift engine driver Albert Lockyer, whose age at the time was in excess of 65, stayed by his generator to make sure that the destroyer had adequate power. The practice was for ships coming into the yard to take their power supply from ashore, since White's generated its own DC current. Unknown to Albert Lockyer, when the raid began the officers aboard the *Blyskawica*, realising that if the yard was hit the ship would lose her source of power, had ordered the onboard generators started to make her self-supporting. Albert Lockyer stayed where he was, at great risk to his life, refusing orders to go to the shelters and little realising that his brave action was not necessary.

Unfortunately, Albert Lockyer's deed, along with countless others at the time, was never recognised. The story of his bravery, though, together with the actions of the crew of the *Blyskawica*, are not forgotten, and the people of Cowes will always remain truly grateful and proud to have been associated with such exceptional courage. In 1982 a plaque was unveiled on The Parade, West Cowes, to commemorate and acknowledge the gallant efforts of the *Blyskawica*. She is now preserved as a memorial and floating museum in the port of Gdynia, Poland.

The *Grom*, though having a less distinctive war career, was nevertheless constantly active, first serving with her sister-ship patrolling the Dutch and Belgian coasts and along the Heligoland Bight during the winter of 1939. Later both were transferred to Rosyth, serving with the battleships *Rodney* and *Valiant* in the Skaggerak, prior to the abortive invasion of Norway. During the Norwegian campaign they were engaged escorting convoys between Bergen and the United Kingdom, and on coastal support duties. On 4 May 1940 the *Grom* was attacked in Rombaksfjord. She sustained direct hits by two bombs and sank rapidly with the loss of 59 of her complement.

The Polish destroyer order was immediately followed by a growing number of Royal Navy ships, the pace of demand for new warships accelerating noticeably as rearmament gathered pace after the Munich Crisis of September 1938. The destroyers *Intrepid* and *Impulsive* were completed in 1937, the sloop *Bittern* and the river gunboat *Scorpion* in 1938, the latter placed on station at Shanghai after being the first of her type to sail out to China under her own steam instead of being shipped out in sections and reassembled there. Up to and just after the outbreak of war the yard completed another sloop, the *Egret*, the patrol vessel *Shearwater,* and two more destroyers, the very similar *Jersey* of the 'Javelin' Class and the *Kingston* of the 'Kelly' Class.

In this period White's also received the order to build the destroyers *Javary* and *Jutahy* for the Brazilian Navy. More or less identical to the Admiralty-designed 'Hero' Class, these vessels were in an advanced state of construction by 3 September 1939. The *Javary* had in fact been launched on the previous 17 July. Immediately war was declared, the Admiralty requisitioned both ships and had them completed to their own requirements as HMS *Havant* and HMS *Havelock*.

The most striking vessel in the shipyard at this time was the 4,000 tons displacement minelayer *Abdiel*, lead ship of a class of six ultra-fast special mine warfare ships. When it seemed that all the superlatives had been exhausted in reference to the Polish destroyers *Grom* and *Blyskawica*, the *Abdiel* set new records for the J. Samuel White shipyard.

Having an overall length of 418 feet, she was the longest ship ever built by White's, so long, in fact, that it was said that while she was on the slipway at East Cowes, her bows protruded over the yard's boundary wall above Clarence Road. The *Abdiel* was also the fastest ship to be built by White's, her turbine engines, with a power output of 72,000 shp, also being the most powerful machinery built by the Engineering Department. Due to the pressing need to get her operational, the *Abdiel* did not undergo formal trials but, unofficially, she achieved a speed in excess of 40 knots.

Abdiel carried between 100 and 150 mines, depending on the type and the nature of the operation being performed. Ironically, she was herself sunk by a mine off Taranto, Italy, on 10 September 1943 after serving as a fast blockade runner relieving the beleaguered Mediterranean island of Malta.

At the outset of war, White's was already working at full capacity on the emergency destroyer contracts placed by the Royal Navy. Having a full order book was, of course, poor compensation for the circumstances that had created it, although even before the political situation had triggered the transfer to defence work, the Company's financial performance had been steadily improving. In 1938, for the first time since 1920, White's paid a dividend on shareholders' ordinary shares.

The final yard improvements prior to the Second World War took the form of two additional slipways constructed by the boat sheds in East Cowes, useful additions well-timed to meet the sudden influx of orders for naval launches and RAF air-sea rescue craft that wartime requirements created.

The transition from peacetime to wartime construction was especially significant to J. Samuel White & Company as it represented a pivotal point linking the Company's busiest peacetime phase of activity and its most productive wartime period.

Below left The first of what are regarded as being the two most superior destroyers built by J. Samuel White & Company, the ORP *Grom*. Both her fine lines and her menacing power can be fully appreciated in this view of her on speed trials. *White's Archives*

Right A deck view of the *Blyskawica*, looking to the stern, while under construction prior to her launch. *White's Archives, Cowes Maritime Museum*

Below The launch of the *Blyskawica* on 1 October 1936. At the top, beyond the tug, is the *Grom*. She has been moved clear, temporarily, while her sister vessel is launched. At the extreme left can be seen the Cowes Harbour Commission floating bridge Number 3, nearing completion. After being withdrawn from service in the 1970s, this floating bridge was towed to Southampton, but foundered in the Solent *en route*. *White's Archives, Cowes Maritime Museum*

WHITE'S OF COWES

Another aerial view of the West Cowes shipyard around 1937/38, showing the filling in of the final part of the quayside to provide continuous straight frontage for fitting-out work. The destroyers *Grom*, *Intrepid*, *Blyskawica* and *Impulsive* can be seen completing. The workshops at the top of the picture were destroyed in German air raids during the Second World War. *White's Archives, Cowes Maritime Museum*

A view of the ORP *Blyskawica*, the famous Polish destroyer remembered with special affection by the townsfolk of Cowes. Her valiant actions on the night of 4 May 1942 were instrumental in saving a large part of the town from being destroyed in a German air raid. *White's Archives*

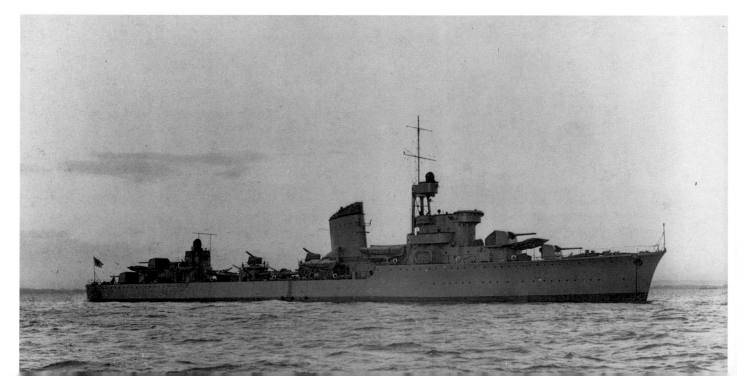

Above HMS *Intrepid* on shipyard trials. The design of the shipyard's flag, flying at the stern, has been changed from the simple letter 'W' and now displays the words 'Whites - Cowes'. *White's Archives*

Below left The launch of the second '*Intrepid*' Class destroyer

HMS *Impulsive*, yard number 1812, on 1 March 1937. *White's Archives, Cowes Maritime Museum*

Below right The Chinese river gunboat *Scorpion* on the stocks just prior to her launch on 20 December 1937. Hats and coats are clearly the order of the day! *White's Archives, Cowes Maritime Museum*

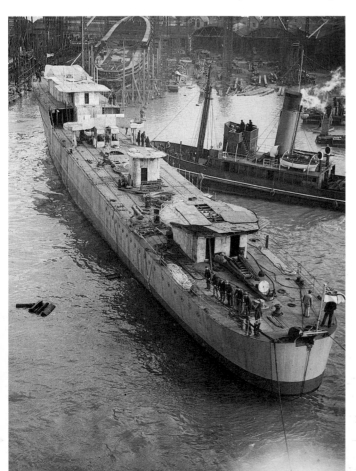

Above The *Seabelle II*, yard number 1647, following her launch on 13 October 1927. *White's Archives, Cowes Maritime Museum*

Left The completed *Seabelle II* alongside the Falcon Shipyard, East Cowes. She was built for the Crown Agents for the Colonies, for service in the Straits Settlements. *White's Archives, Cowes Maritime Museum*

Left White's had its own means of ferrying workmen across the river - a series of motor launches, the first of which was built in 1892. Here a group of workmen are heading towards West Cowes in the 1920s on what is believed to be the *Falcon*, a former Admiralty steam launch. *White's Archives, Bob Saunders collection*

MARITIME HERITAGE

The Joiners' Shop, East Cowes. The Engineer

Workmen on one of the frame-bending machines in the Platers' Shed in the 1930s. *White's Archives, Cowes Maritime Museum*

Propeller shafting in the Turning Shop. *White's Archives, Cowes Maritime Museum*

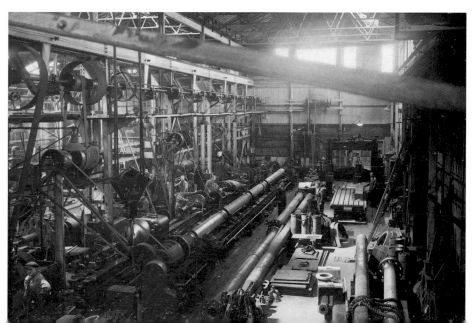

WHITE'S OF COWES

Left One of the yard's design offices, a very cramped working environment compared to its modern equivalent, with the men at the drawing boards in the centre having to stand while they work. *White's Archives, John Durrell collection*

Below The sloop HMS *Egret,* of a modified type, takes to the water on 31 May 1938, with the tug *Hector* in attendance in the foreground. Beside the Submarine Shed, in the background, is the Cowes floating bridge. Out of the picture, to the left, is the old Gridiron Yard in which the first White's floatplanes were constructed. *White's Archives, Cowes Maritime Museum*

MARITIME HERITAGE

Right HMS *Jersey*, a 'Javelin' Class destroyer, one of the last White's-built warships to be completed for the Royal Navy prior to the outbreak of the Second World War. With her single funnel, the *Jersey* presents for the first time the look of the modern destroyer. She lasted for less than two years, falling victim to an enemy mine at the entrance to Grand Harbour, Valletta, Malta, in May 1941. *White's Archives*

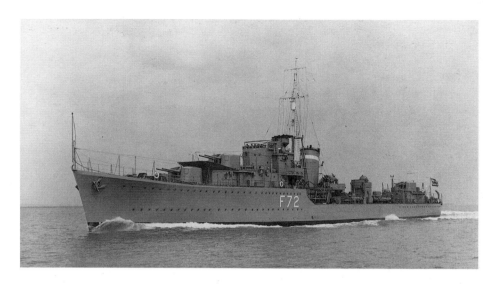

Left Launch of the 'Kelly' Class destroyer *Kingston* on 9 January 1939. The tug *Neptune,* which assisted at many launchings at White's, has already secured the stern lines. *White's Archives, Cowes Maritime Museum*

Below The passenger cargo vessel *Bakar*, yard number 1704, was the second of a pair of vessels for the Yugoslav Company Jadranska Plovidba. Her sistership was the *Rab*. *White's Archives, Cowes Maritime Museum*

5. SECOND WORLD WAR PRODUCTION

In the Second World War production output again comprised both warships and aircraft work, with the emphasis on shipbuilding. Complete aircraft were not built during this conflict, only components which included quantities of Spitfire fuselages, Mosquito undercarriages and Lancaster tailplanes. As in the Great War, the J. Samuel White & Co shipyard earned praise for the quantity and speed of output as well as the high quality of workmanship. On average a new vessel of one type or another was delivered every 4-5 weeks. Output of warships was as follows:

Destroyers (total 26)

Kingston	*Eggesford*
Havant (ex-*Javary*)	*Stevenstone*
Havelock (ex-*Jutahy*)	*Talybont*
Quorn	*Success* (re *Stord*)
Southdown	*Swift*
Silverton (re *Karakowiak*)	*Vixen* (re *Sioux*)
Puckeridge	*Volage*
Southwold	*Cavalier*
Tetcott	*Carysfort*
Quentin	*Contest*
Quiberon	*Crispin* (ex-*Craccher*)
Quickmatch	*Creole* *
Easton	*Scorpion* *

* ships launched after the cessation of hostilities

Minelayer (total 1)

Abdiel

Patrol Vessel (total 1)

Shearwater

Steel Guard Boat (total 1)

Grey Goose

Tank Landing Craft (total 3)

LCT 7034
LCT 4128
LCT 4129

Miscellaneous small craft (total 285)

White's total Second World War production:
317 ships

As in the First World War there were losses among the Royal Navy ships built by White's, rather more than in the previous conflict and no fewer than 17 of the larger classes of ship.

The first casualty was the sloop *Bittern*, bombed by German Heinkel aircraft on 30 April 1940 while lying in Namsos Fjord. The bomb hits caused the detonation of her own depth charges and the doomed vessel was scuttled by British torpedoes after her crew had been removed.

Just over a month later the *Havant* was the next loss while assisting the evacuation at Dunkerque. Her search for survivors close inshore was dramatically terminated on 1 June 1940 when Dornier warplanes bombed and sank her.

Left HMS *Abdiel*, the largest, fastest and most powerful warship built by J. Samuel White, seen here painted in a camouflage colour scheme. The contrast and deep tones of the colours of the scheme would suggest that it is an example of the Admiralty Dark Disruptive pattern. *World Ship Photo Library, Naval Collection*

Above right A deck scene during the construction of the Brazilian destroyer *Javary*, eventually completed for the Royal Navy as HMS *Havant*. In the background is the destroyer HMS *Jersey* completing at West Cowes. *White's Archives, Cowes Maritime Museum*

Right Lowering the boilers into the *Javary*, later HMS *Havant*, on 26 July 1939. *White's Archives, Cowes Maritime Museum*

HMS *Jersey* was the victim of a mine in the entrance to Grand Harbour, Malta, on 2 May 1941. For a time her wreck blocked the channel into the harbour.

In 1942 there were six sinkings. The worst was the torpedoing of the veteran First World War destroyer *Vortigern* on 15 March 1942 while on convoy duty in the North Sea; seven officers and 140 ratings were killed. Prior to this the gunboat *Scorpion* had been deliberately scuttled at Singapore to prevent her capture by the Japanese.

The new 'Hunt' Class destroyer *Southwold* was sunk nine days later, following the Battle of Sirte. She too was mined off Malta while screening the bomb-damaged auxiliary *Breconshire*. At the time she was under the command of Commander C. T. Jellicoe, nephew of the famous Admiral of the Fleet, Earl Jellicoe, commander of the Grand Fleet at the Battle of Jutland.

Another of the First World War 'V' Class destroyers, HMS *Vampire*, transferred to the Royal Australian Navy, was bombed and sunk, with the aircraft carrier *Hermes*, by Japanese aircraft on 9 April 1942.

HMS *Kingston*, the first destroyer to be completed by White's after the beginning of the war, was bombed and sunk in drydock at Malta on 11 April 1942. From the outbreak of war the sloop *Niger* had been operated as a fleet minesweeper, and on 6 July 1942 she was mined and sunk while performing these duties off Iceland.

The year ended with the sinking of the destroyer *Quentin* on 2 December 1942. She was sunk by aircraft-launched torpedoes while returning from attacking an Italian convoy bound for Tunisia.

Four more White's-built ships were sunk in 1943. On 27 August the escort vessel *Egret* was blown up by a German glider bomb off north-west Spain with the loss of six officers and 188 members of the crew.

The other three casualties came in the month of September. The *Puckeridge* was lost on the 6th, torpedoed by a German submarine in the Western Mediterranean; 61 of her crew died. The minelayer *Abdiel* was a mine victim on the 10th, as already described. HMS *Intrepid* was another victim of aerial attack when German aircraft sank her in the harbour of Leros, a Greek island

in the Aegean Sea, on 26 September.

The destroyer *Fury* was a unit in the very large fleet of warships which took part in the D-day landings in France on 6 June 1944. Fifteen days later, while still operating off the beach-head, she struck a mine and was driven ashore in a gale and wrecked. Three days later HMS *Swift* was lost in the same vicinity, another mine casualty. Finally the destroyer *Quorn* was also sunk off the coast of Normandy while guarding the lines of communication to the invasion forces. She was struck by a human torpedo with heavy loss of life, four officers and 126 ratings.

War damage was also inflicted on the shipyard on three occasions. On 28 April 1942 an early morning raid by a small number of Messerschmidt fighter bombers resulted in the total destruction of one of the boat shops. The Polish destroyer *Blyskawica*, which was lying alongside the works at the time, had a narrow escape from serious damage as bombs fell very close to her side. A jetty carrying the ship's gangway was destroyed, the gangway itself being blown into the air and crashing down across the ship but causing only superficial damage.

The intensive air raid of the night of 4 and 5 May 1942, in which some 200 tons of bombs were dropped on the Cowes area, caused widespread damage to Cowes despite the stalwart resistance of the *Blyskawica*, as already described. Saunders-Roe's Solent Works in Medina Road was totally destroyed. In the shipyard, on the same side of the river, a high explosive bomb fell on the quayside causing considerable damage to the nearby buildings. At the southern end of the Falcon Yard and in the Clarence Boatyard in East Cowes incendiary bombs wreaked havoc, resulting in the loss of the Joiners' Shop, Sawmills, Mould Loft and several other buildings. In all, 100,000 square feet of shipyard buildings were destroyed.

Production at the shipyard had suffered disruptions through air-raid warnings right from the beginning of the war, as well as from the need to observe black-out conditions. Even in the daytime, problems existed in the workshops through the loss of daylight, resulting from the painting over of acres of windows, but at night it was not permissible to provide sufficient light to carry on work in the berths after darkness; this imposed a constraint on the number of hours that could be worked. It was vital, therefore, to repair quickly the damage of the May 1942 air raid in order to restore the shipyard's already restricted production capacity.

This began almost straight away, with the clearance of all the devastated buildings. Meanwhile, in an attempt to maintain as high a level of output as possible for the duration of the repairs, accommodation for the affected departments was requisitioned elsewhere on the Isle of Wight. Large manufacturing sheds along the southern perimeter of Parkhurst Forest were among the dispersed premises taken over. Alongside these were hangar buildings used by the Saunders-Roe Repair Section, similarly dislocated, which were later occupied in the postwar period by another White's subsidiary Company, J. Arthur Dixon Limited.

Barely a month after the raid, the wreckage of the bomb-damaged workshops had been cleared, allowing the construction of new shops to commence. Amazingly, by March 1943 most of the lost facilities had been fully

Top left HMS *Havant*, completed and ready for service with the Royal Navy in the war with Germany. As her design was based closely on the 'Hero' Class, she and her sister-ship *Havelock*, also building at White's, were readily adaptable for Admiralty service. *White's Archives*

Far left Laying the first keel plate of the Brazilian destroyer *Jutahy*. The wording on the plate indicates that the ceremony was performed by Mrs Jose-Maria Neiva on 31 May 1938. The *Jutahy* was completed as HMS *Havelock*. *White's Archives, Cowes Maritime Museum*

Above left Bomb damage at the shipyard. The former Falcon Inn at the corner of Bridge Road and Medina Road had been taken over by the Company as part of its office premises. Gutted during the air raid of 4 May 1942, it was demolished and an extension to the Company's main offices, to the left, was built in its place. *White's Archives, Cowes Maritime Museum*

Left Devastation to the lifeboat-building shop in the West Cowes Shipyards (in the background are houses in Pelham Road). A new lifeboat shop was constructed in this area following the clearance of rubble. *White's Archives, Cowes Maritime Museum*

Left HMS *Contest*, a 'Cossack' Class destroyer, was the first all-welded warship to be built for the Royal Navy. Sections of the ship can be seen being constructed in this general view of the Welding Shop. *White's Archives, Cowes Maritime Museum*

Right Laying out the *Contest*'s lines in the new Mould Loft, East Cowes, which was completely rebuilt following the destruction of the original building, with the Main Boat Shop underneath, during the bombing of May 1942. The size of the Mould Loft, in which it was possible to lay out a destroyer full size, is quite evident in this view. *White's Archives, Cowes Maritime Museum*

Below HMS *Contest*, the Royal Navy's first all-welded destroyer. *White's Archives*

reinstated, the new Mould Loft, especially, being a source of pride to the civil engineers and tradesmen engaged in the work. To all concerned it symbolised triumph over adversity, the shipyard's production having been able to continue at maximum capacity with hardly an interruption. The main inconvenience caused to the shipyard's war-building programme by the bombing, apart from some relatively minor delays, had been the total destruction of a quantity of craft in the boatshops.

A third attack during the night of 15 and 16 May 1944 resulted in only slight damage to the shipyard which was quickly repaired.

A development at this time that threatened to complicate the restoration of the shipyard was the decision to undertake the construction of the first all-welded destroyer for the Royal Navy, HMS *Contest*. This required the setting up of a Welding Department in the East Cowes works at the very time when all the available civil engineering plant and workmen were already hard pressed rebuilding the Main Boat Shop and Mould Loft.

The Company's approach to producing welded ships involved the pre-fabrication of sections of up to 8 tons in weight, erecting them upside down in a covered workshop prior to rotating them and transferring them to the slipway for assembly. This dictated the need for a large, clear construction area with adequate space for handling and moving a number of sections in various stages of fabrication, and equipped with overhead travelling cranes of appropriate lifting capacity. Much specialised welding equipment also had to be procured both for use in the

workshops and on the building berths. Besides the logistical problems that this development introduced, there were also technical difficulties to overcome. The welding process could cause shrinkage stresses, creating alignment and fit problems both in the fabrication of a section and in the assembly of a number of sections.

As an indication of how well all these issues were tackled, HMS *Contest* entered the water on 16 December 1944, less than 18 months after the agreement with the Admiralty had been concluded. The destroyers that followed were also manufactured by this process.

When the war ended, it was hoped that the welding facility would provide the Company with a competitive edge in the pursuit of new work, as once again the transition from naval to commercial orders took place. In this context the air-raid damage of May 1942 was, perhaps, a blessing in disguise, for it too ensured that the Company had at least some modern facilities available to them to help confront this new challenge of the return to peacetime trading conditions.

The steel Guard Boat *Grey Goose* was built for a special clandestine war operation. Commanded by Sir Peter Scott, the artist and founder of the Wild Fowl Trust, she was used for secret high-speed runs to Sweden to collect consignments of ball-bearings, essential to the British war manufacturing effort. The ship was a one-off, due in part to her unique purpose but also because a vessel of this type required a specialist shipbuilder to undertake her construction. In the case of White's, this effort was achieved at the expense of destroyer construction, a sacrifice that could not be repeated. *White's Archives, Cowes Maritime Museum*

HMS *Carysfort*, a '*Caesar*' Class destroyer. Her White's-built sister-ship HMS *Cavalier* has been preserved as an example of a typical 'C' Class Second World War destroyer. After a period berthed in Southampton's Ocean Dock she is now undergoing an overhaul at Hartlepool. *R. P. de Kerbrech Collection*

Work under way in the Welding Shop on large sections of the destroyer HMS *Creole*, a '*Crescent*' Class Emergency Flotilla destroyer. *White's Archives, Cowes Maritime Museum*

MARITIME HERITAGE

6. DECLINE AND CLOSURE

With the benefit of the experience of having already converted once from wartime to peacetime operations, after the First World War, the Company felt confident in its ability to adjust to the changed circumstances brought about by the cessation of hostilities in 1945. In marked contrast to the gloomy prewar years of the Depression, the immediate postwar period was one distinguished by a collective optimism and great hope for a better future earned by the sacrifices made through the preceding six years.

Again, almost all the outstanding naval orders were rapidly cancelled, depriving J. Samuel White's of five destroyer contracts, the *Sword* and *Musket* of the 'Weapon' Class, the *Grafton* and *Greyhound* of the 'Gallant' Class, and one of the two 'Daring' Class ships, the *Dervish*. As it turned out, HMS *Dainty*, the remaining 'Daring' Class ship, became the last true destroyer to be built by White's.

Painful though these cancellations were, this had been anticipated and the Company again concentrated its efforts on securing contracts for merchant vessels as shipping companies made good the losses of the war years, as well as contracts for the refurbishment of naval vessels worn out by long years of arduous wartime duties.

In both respects the shipyard was fairly successful and it became possible, over a period of some years, to maintain a reasonably healthy order book for a variety of types of vessel. A period similar to, but better than, that which the Company had experienced between the wars seemed in prospect. As things turned out, however, barely 15 years after the war's end, at the very time that the shipbuilding industry was entering a world recession, the Company became trapped in a downward spiral as the level of work it was able to secure became inadequate to support the entire shipyard. Increasingly it became a fight for survival as orders fell in the face of fierce competition from foreign, predominantly Far Eastern, shipyards - a familiar story for many British shipbuilders.

Back in 1945 this dire situation was still some way off, though, and it is unlikely that any clairvoyant could have accurately predicted then what the future was destined to bring. With Japan, Germany, Italy and France all trying to recover from the near total eradication of their industrial infrastructure, the immediate postwar years were something of a honeymoon period for British companies during which they virtually monopolised the demand for heavy and light engineering manufacture.

Not that White's sat on its laurels. The Company set about implementing a scheme for the modification of the building berths in order to build merchant vessels of the maximum possible length and beam. Naval ships, by comparison, have a much greater length to beam ratio and a shipyard laid out for naval work does not readily lend itself to the volume production of merchant ships. As part of this modernisation programme the shipyard cranes were upgraded. Some were reconditioned, some moved from East to West Cowes, and others, of the latest design, were newly installed.

At the helm through this twilight era for J. Samuel White's was Sir James A. Milne who had joined the firm as a Director in 1941 and who was Company Chairman from 1947 to 1965.

An early order was for two cargo ships for the Société Générale Transports Maritimes à Vapeur, named *Sidi Mabrouk* and *Sidi Okba*. In 1949 the similar *Rio Quequen* (ex-*Artico*) and *Rio Santiago* (ex-*Antarctico*) were built for the Argentine Government, while the twin-screw ferry *Eket* was completed for the West Africa Lighterage and Transport Company (Elder Dempster Limited) for service in West Africa.

In 1950 White's received a five-year contract from the RNLI to build 20 lifeboats. In the same year the destroyer *Dainty* was launched, and a cross-Solent cargo vessel was built for the J. Samuel White subsidiary, the Island Transport Company. The following year saw the completion of the 100th lifeboat built in the yards, the 52-foot Barnett Type *Hilton Briggs*, which went to the Aberdeen Station.

With the emphasis of new building work re-focused on mercantile construction, the Company's attitude to naval work was largely concentrated on conversion orders, which kept the building berths free, tying up only the West Cowes fitting-out quays. Throughout the 1950s White's was renowned for its proficiency in converting former destroyers into frigates, and it undertook numerous contracts of this sort. For the Royal Navy the Company took in hand the *Volage*, built by it in 1944, the *Undaunted* and the *Troubridge*. The *Quantock* and *Meynell* were similarly converted for the Government of Equador, the *Myngs* for the Egyptian Navy, and the *Charity* for Pakistan.

In July 1951 the *Kadoura* was launched for Chargeurs Reunis, and in August the new naval fast patrol boat *Bold Pioneer* attained a speed of 40 knots on her trials.

The *Bold Pioneer* was in fact the Royal Navy's first combined gas turbine and diesel powered vessel. Her sister, the *Bold Pathfinder*, was built by Vospers at Portsmouth. The pair were initially fitted with Metropolitan Vickers gas turbine engines coupled with Mercedes Benz diesels, but the latter units were later replaced with Napier Deltic marine diesel machinery. Although sisters, there were differences between the vessels, principally in their hull design. The *Bold Pioneer* was of hard chine construction, whereas the *Bold Pathfinder* had a rounded hull.

Smaller vessels completed during the first half of the 1950s included a lightship for the Calcutta Port Trust, the pilot vessel *Matthew Flinders* for Brisbane, Australia, and the survey vessel *Pathfinder* for the Crown Agents.

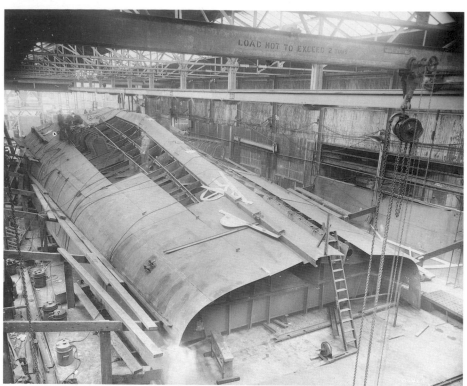

Left A large keel section for the destroyer *Dainty* under construction in the Welding Shop prior to assembly on the slipway. *White's Archives, Cowes Maritime Museum*

Below Launch of HMS *Dainty* on 16 August 1950, the only ship of the 'Daring' Class and the last true destroyer to be built by the Company. *White's Archives, Cowes Maritime Museum*

Right A trials view aboard HMS *Dainty* executing a high-speed turn; her starboard side deck is awash as she goes through the manoeuvre. On board when the photograph was taken was Mervyn Pearson who painted the cover picture and who was at the time a shipyard fitter. *Photographer unknown*

Above far right HMS *Dainty*, last of a select line, the final destroyer built by J Samuel White & Company. *Crown Copyright*

Right Launch of the French cargo ship *Sidi Mabrouk*, yard number 1944, on 24 April 1948. *White's Archives, Cowes Maritime Museum*

MARITIME HERITAGE

Above The Argentine cargo vessel *Artico*, yard number 1958, was launched on 2 December 1948. Prior to delivery she was renamed *Rio Quequen*. She was withdrawn from service in 1978. *White's Archives, Cowes Maritime Museum*

Above The *Artico* completing at West Cowes. Note the workmen filing aboard her at the start of a new workshift. *White's Archives, Cowes Maritime Museum*

Left The launching ceremony in progress for the Chargeurs Reunis fruit carrier *Kadoura*, yard number 1966, on 5 July 1951. *White's Archives, Cowes Maritime Museum*

Below The *Dainty* and *Kadoura*, on the inside, fitting out at West Cowes. *David Marshall*

Above The frigate HMS *Volage* following her conversion from a destroyer. She was built originally by White's in 1944. *White's Archives*

Right The experimental fast patrol boat or 'pocket destroyer' HMS *Bold Pioneer*. Though not as fast as had been hoped, this 122-foot-long craft and her class-mate *Bold Pathfinder*, built by Vospers, were useful vessels from which many valuable lessons were learned about the design and performance of high-speed craft. Most importantly, they highlighted the devastating effect of sea-water and salt spray drawn into engine air intakes, experience that assisted later designers of hovercraft and other fast marine craft. *World Ship Photo Library, Naval Collection*

New frigates were also built by White's. Five ships of the small 'Blackwood' Class Type 14 frigates were constructed, the *Dundas*, *Exmouth* and *Grafton* for the Royal Navy, and the *Khukri* and *Kuthar* for the Indian Navy; the latter was yard number 2000 on the Company's main yard list. Later HMS *Exmouth* was converted into an experimental gas turbine ship for the Admiralty, which resulted in her being fitted with a modified, tapering funnel by which she could be distinguished from the other ships of her Class.

Two 'Rothesay' Class Type 12 frigates were also completed by White's, HMS *Londonderry* in 1959 and the Royal New Zealand Navy's *Taranaki* in 1960. The shipyard's penultimate frigate for the Royal Navy was the twin-funnelled 'Tribal' Class general purpose type, *Eskimo*.

An interesting incident involved the Company on 10 December 1957 in connection with the launching of the Constants Limited's cargo vessel *Susan Constant*. The tug *Tampeon*, with Red Funnel's *Neptune*, was on station to take control of the cargo ship as she came off the slipway, to arrest her movement toward the West Cowes quay wall. During the manoeuvres, which the restricted width of the River Medina at this point made particularly tricky to execute, the *Tampeon* ended up, high and dry, on the chains of the floating bridge, bringing all traffic between the two sides of the town to a standstill.

In 1954 J. Samuel White acquired the Scottish shipbuilding firm of William Weatherhead & Sons. Two years later the Company purchased the Cowes rope manufacturer Henry Bannister as part of a continuing programme of expansion and diversification. Even as the 1950s were progressing to a close, though, there were already signs of a downturn in yard activity, so it came as a welcome boost to the rather depleted order book when two substantial and interesting contracts were obtained in 1958.

The first of these was for four large lighthouse tenders for the Corporation of Trinity House for delivery between

HMS *Londonderry*, launched by Viscountess Brookeborough on 20 May 1958. *White's Archives, Ron Trowell*

1960 and 1963. They were striking little ships, some 220 feet in length, their long foredeck dominated by a heavy, mast-mounted jib hoist for lifting and lowering navigation buoys. The lead ship *Mermaid*, was followed in turn by the *Siren*, *Stella* and *Winston Churchill*. These vessels remain afloat, the last two having only left Trinity House service in recent years.

In parallel with the Trinity House contract, White's received the British Transport Commission's order for two cross-Channel passenger ferries. Named *Caesarea* and *Sarnia*, they entered the Channel Islands service from Weymouth in 1961 and 1962 respectively.

The worldwide slump in shipbuilding began seriously to affect the Company from early in 1961. The possibility of obtaining new orders for Admiralty vessels, to keep both the shipbuilding and engineering sides of the Company in business, became more and more remote. In March 1961 140 men were laid off, the first of an increasing number of redundancies in the yard.

During 1962, rather inexplicably given the Company's worsening financial situation, the redundant gas works site at West Cowes was purchased. Situated alongside the shipyard's southern boundary, it permitted the building of a wooden extension to the fitting-out quays.

To keep the wheels turning in the shipyard, strenuous efforts were made by the Company to obtain work. This effort resulted in orders for refitting the Egyptian destroyers *El Fateh* and *El Kaher*, contracts for North Sea oil rig support vessels, and an order for the 'Leander' Class frigate *Arethusa*, the last ship to be built by White's for the Royal Navy, ending a tradition which went back 269 years.

In spite of this there were continuing difficulties, and in 1964 the Boatbuilding Department was closed down; the final products of the boat sheds were 11 motor whalers for the Royal Navy. The last RNLI lifeboat, the Oakley Type *William Henry and Mary King,* was delivered to her station at Cromer, Norfolk, in October 1964.

In July 1965 the frigate *Arethusa* was completed, the final phase of construction being supervised by the engineering staff since all the shipbuilding management had left the Company the previous April. It had now become obvious that the closing of the shipyard and the end of J. Samuel White & Company as a shipbuilding concern was inevitable.

Shipbuilding ceased altogether at East Cowes in November 1965 and the Falcon shipyard was closed. Although not the last vessel to leave the yards, the supply workboat *South Shore* was the last ship to appear on the main yard list, number 2026.

March 1966 saw the closure of the galvanising shop and the foundry as the rundown of the shipyard began to gather pace. That April the now empty East Cowes premises were sold to the British Hovercraft Corporation, the former Saunders-Roe aircraft manufacturers, by then part of the Westland Group of companies. As a gesture acknowledging the site's long and fascinating history, they retained the shipyard's name and to this day it is still known as the Falcon Works. The building berths were progressively removed and filled in behind a quay wall to provide a large area of hard-standing that was more appropriate to this company's production of hovercraft and aircraft components.

During July 1966 part of the Bannister's rope walk was demolished, the remainder being sold off in 1968; what was left of the rope-making work was transferred to the main factory. The Somerton Works was also closed at this time and the site disposed of in 1969.

Total closure seemed imminent, but the Company was to survive for a few more years by seeking new products on which they could employ the factory machinery and utilise the skills of the remaining workforce, products such as propulsion units for shipboarding equipment and air-conditioners. These, coupled with a number of existing product lines which were still profitable, among them steam turbines for Royal Navy ships, tided the Company over for five years. However, late in 1969 the production of steam turbines, which was rather labour-intensive, was dealt a death blow when the Admiralty decided to abandon steam engines in favour of gas turbines. The situation became acute, given that a further economic recession was starting, and the Directors were faced with the problem of how to survive.

The initial solution was for J. Samuel White & Company to act as a licensee for the Elliot Company of the United States of America (a subsidiary of the Carrier Corporation that produced compressors and turbines). This arrangement lasted to January 1972 when the entire Company, such as it remained, was taken over by the Carrier Corporation. The continuing downward direction of White's fortunes now compelled the selling off of its remaining subsidiaries in 1974, including the Island Transport Company, whose value to the Company had been somewhat reduced since the date when shipbuilding had ceased.

On 20 April 1977 the Company name was changed to Elliott Turbomachinery Limited and the name of White, which had been associated with shipbuilding at Cowes for nearly 200 years, disappeared. The deepening world recession continued to cause severe economic problems and in 1981 Elliott's decided to pull out, finally closing the former White's company down after a struggle that had lasted almost 20 years. The West Cowes premises remained more or less empty for some 12 months, but by the end of 1982 several companies, mainly involved in boatbuilding in some way, had occupied the old yards.

Luckily, although the local authority had not been in a position to influence instrumentally the turn of events, it had appreciated the vital importance of the shipyard's heritage as part of the history of Cowes as a whole. Accordingly, assistance was given with the proper disposition of the shipyard records and archives, ensuring the permanent retention of the majority at the Cowes

Maritime Museum and in the Isle of Wight Records Office at Newport.

Of greater importance, the authority resurrected the shipyard name after an interval of only five years, guaranteeing for posterity its continued association with Cowes. When, in 1982, the former shipyard premises in West Cowes were reorganised as an industrial estate, it was given the name Samuel Whites Estate. This was partly in recognition of the continued involvement of the majority of the estate's businesses with marine affairs, but it was mainly as a testament to the White family of Broadstairs, Kent, whose enterprise and endeavours through several generations had served the town so well, and to the shipyard of that name that had accounted for the lion's share of the town's trade and commerce for almost two centuries.

The launch of the lightship *Flame*, built for the Calcutta Port Trust. *White's Archives, Cowes Maritime Museum*

Top left The motor barge *XXXX* built in 1948 for the brewery W. B. Mew Langton. This reveals that long before drinkers of Castlemaine lager 'wouldn't give a XXXX for anything else', another beer-related product had carried this unusual identity! *R. P. de Kerbrech*

Above 'Blackwood' Class frigate HMS *Exmouth*, launched on 16 November 1955 by Lady Creasey. *White's Archives, Ron Trowell*

Left Welding a keel section for HMS *Grafton*. *White's Archives, Ron Trowell*

Below HMS *Grafton* broadside on with the East Cowes shipyard and slipways as a backdrop. *White's Archives, Ron Trowell*

Right The 350-foot-long cargo ship *Susan Constant*, built for Constants Limited of Cardiff, on the slipway prior to her launch. *White's Archives, Ron Trowell*

Above The launch of the *Susan Constant*, yard number 1996, by Mrs Margaret Constant on 10 December 1957. The tug *Neptune* has the newly launched vessel under control; meanwhile, out of the picture, behind the photographer, the second tug, *Tampeon*, has come to grief on the chains of the Cowes floating bridge. *Photographer unknown*

Right The Lifeboat Shop, West Cowes, with craft at various stages of construction. *White's Archives, Ron Trowell*

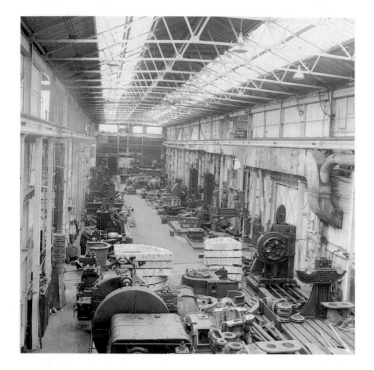

Top left The long 'A' Shop, Heavy Machine Shop, in the 1950s.

Top right The Boiler Shop at the same time, little changed from almost half a century earlier.

Above left Turbine assembly in progress in the Turbine Shop.

Above right The boilers being placed aboard the Indian Navy frigate *Khukri* on 15 July 1956.

Right The Light Machine Shop, packed tight with machinery and, apparently, a very noisy workplace. The exposed drive belts, today prohibited, are evidence of the progress in industrial safety in just over 25 years. *All photos White's Archives, Ron Trowell*

Right The Marine Society training vessel *Earl of Romney* built in 1958 as the inshore survey vessel HMS *Echo*, and one of a dwindling number of White's-built vessels still afloat. With two other similar vessels, the Marine Society provides sea training courses for the Royal and Merchant Naval Services as well as many other national maritime organisations. The author's son participated in a leadership course aboard this ship in January 1993 as a Prospective Officer Candidate for the Royal Navy.

The Marine Society was founded in 1756 to encourage men and boys to join the Royal Navy, and since that time has been actively involved in maintaining the highest standards of sea training. *The Marine Society*

Above General view of the Falcon Shipyard with, on the slipways from left to right, the Trinity House lighthouse tender *Siren*, the Royal New Zealand Navy frigate *Taranaki*, the Trinity House lighthouse tender *Mermaid*, one day prior to her launch, and the cross-Channel steamer *Caesarea* in the early stages of construction. *White's Archives, Ron Trowell*

Right The launch of the Trinity House ship *Mermaid* on 26 March 1959 by Mrs O. E. Noakes. *White's Archives, Ron Trowell*

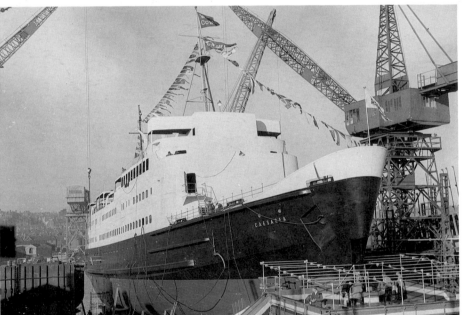

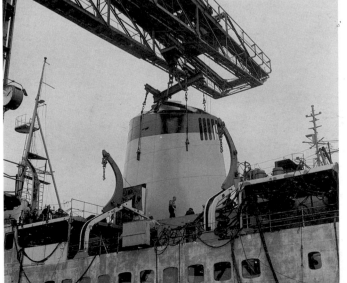

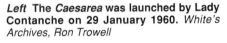

Above left A close-up view of the frigate *Taranaki*'s fore section, on the slipway on 2 July 1959. *White's Archives, Ron Trowell*

Above The British Transport Commission's passenger steamer *Caesarea* under construction on 31 August 1959. *White's Archives, Ron Trowell*

Left The *Caesarea* was launched by Lady Contanche on 29 January 1960. *White's Archives, Ron Trowell*

Left Shipping aboard the *Caesarea*'s funnel on 17 June 1960. *White's Archives, Ron Trowell*

Above right The *Caesarea*, on the left, and the *Sarnia*, showing how their hull colouring was changed after experimentation to determine the most pleasing appearance - compare this photograph with the views of the *Caesarea* opposite and the *Sarnia* below. *White's Archives, Ron Trowell*

Right The cross-Channel steamer *Sarnia*, yard number 2009, on trials on 13 May 1961. *White's Archives, Ron Trowell*

MARITIME HERITAGE

Above Gas turbine and (*left*) steam turbine machinery under construction for HMS *Eskimo*, October 1961. *White's Archives, Ron Trowell*

Below Transferring a luffing crane from East Cowes to West Cowes on 24 November 1962 with the aid of the Port of Southampton's giant floating crane. HMS *Eskimo* can be seen in the background. *White's Archives, Ron Trowell*

81

Left HMS *Eskimo* on trials. *White's Archives, Ron Trowell*

Above The 'Leander' Class frigate HMS *Arethusa*, the last Royal Navy ship to be built by J. Samuel White's, taking shape on the slipway. *White's Archives, Ron Trowell*

Left A large hull section for HMS *Arethusa* under construction in the Welding Shop. *White's Archives, Ron Trowell*

Right The former J. Samuel White main office in 1992, now part of the Samuel White Industrial Estate, providing accommodation for a wide diversity of businesses, including boatbuilders, a microwave oven parts supplier, a computer company and a marine support and towage concern. *David L. Williams*

MARITIME HERITAGE

Right HMS *Arethusa* in service. Her departure from the shipyard closed an era that had commenced 270 years earlier, in 1695, with the commencement of the first ship built at Cowes for the Royal Navy. *World Ship Photo Library, Naval Collection*

Left One of the final ships to be built by White's was yard number 2025, the motor coaster *Crescence*, launched on 23 October 1964 for the London & Rochester Trading Company. *World Ship Photo Library*

The former J. Samuel White shipyard premises as they are today. In East Cowes, on the far side of the River Medina, the Westland Aerospace Falcon Works has been extensively reconstructed and modernised for the production of high-tech composite aircraft components for the world's major long-haul and regional airliners. In the foreground, the West Cowes shipyard is still largely recognisable as it was when White's closed down. A new covered assembly shop on the right, owned by FBM Marine, indicates that even here the appearance of the old shipyard is now changing as the requirements of new industries lead to the demolition of old buildings and the erection of modern replacements. Even so,

APPENDIX 1
MAJOR NAVAL VESSELS BUILT
1885-1963

Note: Under 'Date', 'd' is the delivery date and 'l' the launch date

Yard No	Name	Type	Owner	Date
40	*Swift*	Torpedo Boat	Royal Navy	d 1885
83		HM Torpedo Boat No 34	Royal Navy	d 8/1886
84		HM Torpedo Boat No 35	Royal Navy	d 1/1887
85		HM Torpedo Boat No 36	Royal Navy	d 2/1887
86		HM Torpedo Boat No 37	Royal Navy	d 2/1887
87		HM Torpedo Boat No 38	Royal Navy	d 3/1887
46	*Sea Serpent*	Torpedo Boat	Royal Navy	l 03/10/87
53	*Mahrata*	Torpedo Boat	India Office	d 1888
54	*Sikh*	Torpedo Boat	India Office	d 1888
55	*Rajput*	Torpedo Boat	India Office	d 1888
10		HM Torpedo Boat No 94	Royal Navy	l 27/07/93
11		HM Torpedo Boat No 95	Royal Navy	d 1894
12		HM Torpedo Boat No 96	Royal Navy	d 1894
45	*Conflict*	Destroyer ('A' Class)	Royal Navy	l 13/12/94
46	*Teazer*	Destroyer ('A' Class)	Royal Navy	l 09/02/95
47	*Wizard*	Destroyer ('A' Class)	Royal Navy	l 26/02/95
155		HM Torpedo Boat No 114	Royal Navy	l 08/06/03
156		HM Torpedo Boat No 115	Royal Navy	l 19/11/03
157		HM Torpedo Boat No 116	Royal Navy	l 21/12/03
158		HM Torpedo Boat No 117	Royal Navy	l 18/02/04
199	*Ness*	Destroyer ('River' or 'E' Class)	Royal Navy	l 05/01/05
200	*Nith*	Destroyer ('River' or 'E' Class)	Royal Navy	l 07/03/05
223	*Cricket*	Coastal Destroyer	Royal Navy	l 23/01/06

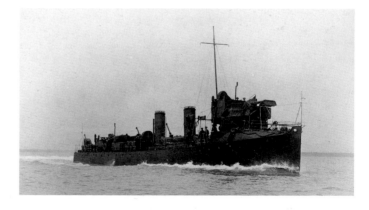

A coastal destroyer of the '*Cricket*' Class. These vessels were later redesignated as First Class Torpedo Boats. *White's Archives*

Yard No	Name	Type	Owner	Date
224	*Dragonfly*	Coastal Destroyer	Royal Navy	l 13/03/06
225	*Firefly*	Coastal Destroyer	Royal Navy	l 01/09/06
226	*Sandfly*	Coastal Destroyer	Royal Navy	l 30/10/06
227	*Spider*	Coastal Destroyer	Royal Navy	l 15/12/06
228	*Mohawk*	Destroyer ('Tribal' or 'F' Class)	Royal Navy	l 15/03/07
253		HM Coastal Destroyer No 13	Royal Navy	l 10/07/07
254		HM Coastal Destroyer No 14	Royal Navy	l 26/09/07
255		HM Coastal Destroyer No 15	Royal Navy	l 19/11/07

Yard No	Name	Type	Owner	Date
1256		HM Coastal Destroyer No 16	Royal Navy	l 23/12/07
1257	*Saracen*	Destroyer ('Tribal' or 'F' Class)	Royal Navy	l 31/03/08
1271		HM Coastal Destroyer No 25	Royal Navy	l 28/07/08
1272		HM Coastal Destroyer No 26	Royal Navy	l 28/08/08
1273		HM Coastal Destroyer No 27	Royal Navy	l 29/09/08
1274		HM Coastal Destroyer No 28	Royal Navy	l 29/10/08
1275	*Crusader*	Destroyer ('Tribal' or 'F' Class)	Royal Navy	l 20/03/09
1292	*Harpy*	Destroyer ('Beagle' or 'G' Class)	Royal Navy	l 27/11/09
1293	*Basilisk*	Destroyer ('Beagle' or 'G' Class)	Royal Navy	l 09/02/10
1315	*Redpole*	Destroyer ('Acorn' or 'H' Class)	Royal Navy	l 24/06/10
1316	*Rifleman*	Destroyer ('Acorn' or 'H' Class)	Royal Navy	l 22/08/10
1317	*Ruby*	Destroyer ('Acorn' or 'H' Class)	Royal Navy	l 04/11/10
1322	*Ferrett*	Destroyer ('I' Class)	Royal Navy	l 12/04/11
1323	*Forester*	Destroyer ('I' Class)	Royal Navy	l 01/06/11
1362	*Almirante Lynch*	Flotilla Leader	Chilean Navy	d 1/1914
1363	*Almirante Condell*	Flotilla Leader	Chilean Navy	d 1914
1386	*Faulknor* (ex-*Almirante Simpson*)	Flotilla Leader	Royal Navy	l 26/02/14
1387	*Broke (ex-Almirante Goni)*	Flotilla Leader	Royal Navy	l 25/05/14

'**Acorn**' Class destroyer *Ferrett* showing her distinctive funnels. *White's Archives*

'**M**' Class destroyer *Medina*. *White's Archives*

1388	*Botha (ex-Almirante Williams Robelledo)*	Flotilla Leader	Royal Navy	l 02/12/14
1389	*Tipperary (ex-Almirante Riveros)*	Flotilla Leader	Royal Navy	l 05/03/15
1390	*Laurel (ex-Redgauntlet)*	Destroyer ('Laforey' or 'L' Class)	Royal Navy	l 06/05/13
1391	*Liberty (ex-Rosalind)*	Destroyer ('Laforey' or 'L' Class)	Royal Navy	l 15/09/13
	G15	Submarine	Royal Navy	Cancelled
1446	*Lightfoot*	Flotilla Leader	Royal Navy	l 28/05/15
1455	*Magic (ex-Marigold)*	Destroyer ('M' Class Emergency)	Royal Navy	l 10/09/15
1456	*Moresby (ex-Marlion)*	Destroyer ('M' Class Emergency)	Royal Navy	l 20/11/15
1465	*P11*	Patrol Vessel	Royal Navy	l 14/10/15
1466	*P12*	Patrol Vessel	Royal Navy	l 04/12/15
1467	*Medina (ex-Redmill)*	Destroyer ('M' Class Emergency)	Royal Navy	l 08/03/16
1468	*Medway (ex-Redwing)*	Destroyer ('M' Class Emergency)	Royal Navy	l 19/04/16
1477	*Sable*	Destroyer ('R' Class Emergency)	Royal Navy	l 28/06/16
	E32	Submarine	Royal Navy	l 16/08/16
1478	*Setter*	Destroyer ('R' Class Emergency)	Royal Navy	l 18/08/16
1480	*P40*	Patrol Vessel	Royal Navy	l 12/07/16
1481	*Trenchant*	Destroyer (Modified 'R' Class)	Royal Navy	l 23/12/16
1482	*Tristram*	Destroyer (Modified 'R' Class)	Royal Navy	l 24/02/17
1483	*P52*	Patrol Vessel	Royal Navy	l 28/09/16
1484	*Vampire*	Flotilla Leader (Admiralty V Design)	Royal Navy	l 21/05/17
1484	*P59*	Patrol Vessel	Royal Navy	l 02/11/17
1491	*Vectis*	Destroyer ('V' Class)	Royal Navy	l 04/09/17

1492	*Vortigern*	Destroyer ('V' Class)	Royal Navy	l 15/10/17
Yard No	**Name**	**Type**	**Owner**	**Date**
1493	*Winchelsea*	Destroyer ('W' Class)	Royal Navy	l 15/12/17
1494	*Winchester*	Destroyer ('W' Class)	Royal Navy	l 01/02/18
1496	*PC67*	Patrol Vessel ('Q' ship)	Royal Navy	l 07/05/17
1497	*PC68*	Patrol Vessel ('Q' ship)	Royal Navy	l 29/06/17
	F2	Submarine	Royal Navy	l 07/07/17
1506	*Tribune*	Destroyer ('*Trenchant*' or 'S' Class)	Royal Navy	l 28/03/18
1507	*Trinidad*	Destroyer ('*Trenchant*' or 'S' Class)	Royal Navy	l 08/05/18
1508	*PC71*	Patrol Vessel ('Q' ship)	Royal Navy	l 18/03/18
1509	*PC72*	Patrol Vessel ('Q' ship)	Royal Navy	l 08/06/18
1510	*PC73*	Patrol Vessel ('Q' ship)	Royal Navy	l 01/08/18
1511	*PC74*	Patrol Vessel ('Q' ship)	Royal Navy	l 04/10/18
1512	*Trojan*	Destroyer ('*Trenchant*' or 'S' Class)	Royal Navy	l 20/07/18
1513	*Truant*	Destroyer ('*Trenchant*' or 'S' Class)	Royal Navy	l 18/09/18
1514	*Trusty*	Destroyer ('*Trenchant*' or 'S' Class)	Royal Navy	l 06/11/18

HMS *Trusty* belching smoke and creating a huge bow wave as she is put through her paces on trials. *White's Archives*

1524	*Witherington*	Destroyer (Modified 'W' Class)	Royal Navy	l 16/01/19
1525	*Wivern*	Destroyer (Modified 'W' Class)	Royal Navy	l 16/04/19
1526	*Wolverine*	Destroyer (Modified 'W' Class)	Royal Navy	l 17/07/19
1527	*Worcester*	Destroyer (Modified 'W' Class)	Royal Navy	l 24/10/19
1528	*Wrangler*	Destroyer (Modified 'W' Class)	Royal Navy	Cancelled
1541	*Werewolf*	Destroyer (Modified 'W' Class)	Royal Navy	Cancelled
1542	*Westphal*	Destroyer (Modified 'W' Class)	Royal Navy	Cancelled
1543	*Westward Ho*	Destroyer (Modified 'W' Class)	Royal Navy	Cancelled
1651	*Mendoza*	Destroyer	Argentine Navy	d 1929
1652	*Tucuman*	Destroyer	Argentine Navy	l 16/10/28
1653	*La Rioja*	Destroyer	Argentine Navy	d 1929
1707	*Kempenfelt*	Destroyer ('*Crusader*' or 'C' Class)	Royal Navy	l 29/10/31
1751	*Forester*	Destroyer ('*Fearless*' or 'F' Class)	Royal Navy	l 28/06/34
1752	*Fury*	Destroyer ('*Fearless*' or 'F' Class)	Royal Navy	l 10/09/34
1791	*Niger*	Sloop ('*Halcyon*' Class)	Royal Navy	l 29/01/36
1792	*Salamander*	Sloop ('*Halcyon*' Class)	Royal Navy	l 24/03/36
1800	*Grom*	Destroyer	Polish Navy	l 20/07/36
1801	*Blyskawica*	Destroyer	Polish Navy	l 01/10/39
1811	*Intrepid*	Destroyer ('*Intrepid*' or 'I' Class)	Royal Navy	l 17/12/36
1812	*Impulsive*	Destroyer ('*Intrepid*' or 'I' Class)	Royal Navy	l 01/03/37
1820	*Bittern*	Sloop ('*Bittern*' Class)	Royal Navy	l 14/07/37
1825	*Scorpion*	River Gunboat	Royal Navy	l 20/12/37
1835	*Egret*	Sloop ('*Egret*' Class)	Royal Navy	l 31/05/38
1837	*Jersey*	Destroyer ('*Javelin*' or 'J' Class)	Royal Navy	l 26/09/38
1838	*Kingston*	Destroyer ('*Kelly*' or 'K' Class)	Royal Navy	l 09/01/39
1868	*Havant (ex-Javary)*	Destroyer ('*Hero*' or 'H' Class)	Royal Navy	l 17/07/39
1869	*Havelock (ex-Jutahy)*	Destroyer ('*Hero*' or 'H' Class)	Royal Navy	l 16/10/39
1880	*Shearwater*	Patrol Vessel	Royal Navy	l 18/04/39
1881	*Abdiel*	Minelayer	Royal Navy	l 23/04/40
1882	*Quorn*	Destroyer ('Hunt' Class Group I Atherstone Type)	Royal Navy	l 27/03/40

Yard No	Name	Type	Owner	Date
1883	*Southdown*	Destroyer ('Hunt' Class Group I Atherstone Type)	Royal Navy	05/07/40
1884	*Bee*	River Gunboat	Royal Navy	Cancelled
1899	*Silverton* (re *Karakowiak*)	Destroyer ('Hunt' Class Group II Blankney Type)	Royal Navy	l 04/12/40
1900	*Puckeridge*	Destroyer ('Hunt' Class Group II Blankney Type)	Royal Navy	l 06/03/41
1905	*Southwold*	Destroyer ('Hunt' Class Type II)	Royal Navy	l 29/05/41
1906	*Tetcott*	Destroyer ('Hunt' Class Type II)	Royal Navy	l 12/08/41
1907	*Quentin*	Destroyer ('*Quilliam*' or 'Q' Class Emergency)	Royal Navy	l 05/11/41
1908	*Quiberon*	Destroyer ('*Quilliam*' or 'Q' Class Emergency)	Royal Navy	l 31/01/42
1909	*Quickmatch*	Destroyer ('*Quilliam*' or 'Q' Class Emergency)	Royal Navy	l 11/04/42
1910	Unnamed	Destroyer ('*Black Swan*' Class)	Royal Navy	Cancelled
1911	Unnamed	Destroyer ('*Black Swan*' Class)	Royal Navy	Cancelled
1916	*Easton*	Destroyer ('Hunt' Class Group III Atherstone Type)	Royal Navy	l 11/07/42
1917	*Eggesford*	Destroyer ('Hunt' Class Group III Atherstone Type)	Royal Navy	l 12/09/42
1918	*Stevenstone*	Destroyer ('Hunt' Class Group III Atherstone Type)	Royal Navy	l 23/11/42
1919	*Talybont*	Destroyer ('Hunt' Class Group III Atherstone Type)	Royal Navy	l 03/02/43

HMS *Talybont*, a 'Hunt' Class Group III Atherstone Type destroyer. A trials photograph, showing her working up a smokescreen.
White's Archives, Cowes Maritime Museum

Yard No	Name	Type	Owner	Date
1920	*Grey Goose*	Steel Guard Boat	Royal Navy	l 14/02/42
1921	*Success* (re *Stord*)	Destroyer ('*Savage*' or 'S' Class Emergency)	Royal Navy	l 03/04/43
1922	*Swift*	Destroyer ('*Savage*' or 'S' Class Emergency)	Royal Navy	l 15/06/43
1923	*Vixen* (re *Sioux*)	Destroyer ('*Valentine*' or 'V' Class Emergency)	Royal Navy	l 14/09/43
1924	*Volage*	Destroyer ('*Valentine*' or 'V' Class Emergency)	Royal Navy	l 15/12/43
1925	Unnamed	Destroyer (Modified '*Black Swan*' Class)	Royal Navy	Cancelled
1926	Unnamed	Fleet Destroyer	Royal Navy	Cancelled
1927	Unnamed	Fleet Destroyer	Royal Navy	Cancelled
1928	*Cavalier*	Destroyer ('*Caesar*' or 'C' Class Emergency)	Royal Navy	l 07/04/44
1929	*Carysfort*	Destroyer ('*Caesar*' or 'C' Class Emergency)	Royal Navy	l 25/07/44
1930	*Contest*	Destroyer ('*Cossack*' or 'CO' Class Emergency)	Royal Navy	l 16/12/44

Yard No	Name	Type	Owner	Date
1931	Crispin (ex-Craccher)	Destroyer ('Crescent' or 'CR' Class Emergency)	Royal Navy	l 23/06/45
1932	Creole	Destroyer ('Crescent' or 'CR' Class Emergency)	Royal Navy	l 22/11/45
1933	Scorpion	Destroyer ('Weapon' Class)	Royal Navy	l 15/08/45
1934	Sword	Destroyer ('Weapon' Class)	Royal Navy	Cancelled
1935	Musket	Destroyer ('Weapon' Class)	Royal Navy	Cancelled
1936	LCT 7034	LCT (Mark 3)	Royal Navy	d 1945
1937	Grafton	Destroyer ('Gallant' Class)	Royal Navy	Cancelled
1938	Greyhound	Destroyer ('Gallant' Class)	Royal Navy	Cancelled
1939	LCT 4128	LCT (Mark 8)	Royal Navy	d 1945
1940	LCT 4129	LCT (Mark 8)	Royal Navy	d 1945
1941	Dainty	Destroyer ('Daring' Class)	Royal Navy	l 16/08/50
1942	Dervish	Destroyer ('Daring' Class)	Royal Navy	Cancelled
5415	Bold Pioneer	Fast Patrol Boat	Royal Navy	l 18/08/51
1969	Dundas	Frigate ('Blackwood' Class Type 14)	Royal Navy	l 25/09/53
1970	Exmouth	Frigate ('Blackwood' Class Type 14)	Royal Navy	l 16/11/55
1971	Grafton	Frigate ('Blackwood' Class Type 14)	Royal Navy	l 11/01/57
1987	Khukri	Frigate ('Blackwood' Class Type 14)	Indian Navy	l 20/11/56
1995	Londonderry	Frigate (Modified 'Rothesay' Class Type 12)	Royal Navy	l 20/05/58
2000	Kuthar	Frigate ('Blackwood' Class Type 14)	Indian Navy	l 14/10/58
2001	Eskimo	Frigate ('Tribal' Class Type 81)	Royal Navy	l 20/03/61
2006	Taranaki	Frigate ('Rothesay' Class Type 12)	Royal New Zealand Navy	l 19/08/59
2015	Arethusa	Frigate ('Leander' Class Improved Type 12)	Royal Navy	l 05/11/63

HMS *Grafton* on trials off Cowes, 12 January 1957. *White's Archives, Ron Trowell*

The Indian Navy frigate *Kuthar* on trials off Cowes on 17 July 1959. *White's Archives, Ron Trowell*

APPENDIX 2
RNLI LIFEBOATS BUILT 1898-1964

Key: B = Barnett; L = Liverpool; N&S = Norfolk & Suffolk; O = Oakley; R = Ramsgate; S = Surf; SR = Self Righter; STM = Steam; W = Watson; WB = Watson Beach

Note: Apart from the steam lifeboats, all are motor powered.

Yard No	Off No	Type	Name	Station(s)	
1054	420	STM	*James Stevens No 3*	Grimsby	1898-1903
				Gorleston	1903-1908
				Angle	1908-1915
				Totland	1915-1919
				Dover	1919-1922
				Holyhead	1922-1928
1055	421	STM	*James Stevens No 4*	Padstow	1899-1900
1101	446	STM	*City of Glasgow*	Harwich	1901-1918

Yard No	Off No	Type	Name	Station(s)	
1578	655	SR	*Priscilla Macbean*	Eastbourne	1921-1927
				Kirkudbright	1928-1931
				Maryport	1931-1934
1566	670	N&S	*H. F. Bailey* re *John and Mary Meiklam of Gladswood*	Cromer	1923-1924
				Gorleston	1924-1939
				Relief	1939-1952
1567	671	W	*The Brothers*	Penlee	1922-1931
				Falmouth	1931-1934
				Relief	1934-1948
				Workington	1948-1952
1574	672	SR	*Alfred and Clara Heath*	Brixham	1922-1930
				Salcombe	1931-1938
				Reserve	1938-1940

The steam lifeboat *James Stevens No 3*, based in 1898 at the RNLI station at Grimsby and withdrawn from service at the Holyhead station in 1928. *White's Archives, Cowes Maritime Museum*

The steam lifeboat *Lady Forrest* was constructed for the Western Australian Government in 1903, and is now preserved. It is possible that the man standing on deck in the centre, with a beard and wearing a bowler hat, is John Samuel White. *White's Archives, Cowes Maritime Museum*

Yard No	Off No	Type	Name	Station(s)	
1648	704	R	Greater London (Civil Service No 3) re Ades 1	Southend-on-Sea	1928-1941
				Relief	1941-1945
				Southend-on-Sea	1945-1955
				Relief	1955-1957
1649	705	R	E.M.E.D.	Walton-on-Naze	1928-1953
				Relief	1953-1956
1656	708	W	H.C.J.	Holyhead (temporary)	1928-1929
				Thurso	1929-1956
				Relief	1956-1962
1657	710	W	White Star	Fishguard	1930-1956
				Relief	1956-1968
1662	711	W	James Macfee	Cromarty	1928-1955
				Relief	1955-1959
1663	712	W	C.D.E.C.	Fowey	1928-1954
				Relief	1954-1959
1664	713	W	Elizabeth Elson	Angle	1929-1957
				Relief	1957-1968
1666	716	W	Sarah Ward and William David Crosweller	Courtmacsherry	1929-1957
				Relief	1957-1959
				Whitehills	1959-1961
1669	717	B	A.E.D.	Holyhead	1929-1950
				Valentia	1950-1954
1670	718	B	William and Harriot	Stornoway	1929-1954
				Relief	1954-1959
1671	719	B	Queen Victoria	St Peter Port (Guernsey)	1930-1940
				Killybegs	1941-1945
				St Peter Port	1945-1954
				Relief	1954-1958
1672	720	B	City of Glasgow	Campbeltown	1929-1953
				Relief	1953-1958
1673	721	W	Lady Kylsant	Weymouth	1929-1930
				Howth	1930-1937
				Wicklow	1937-1956
1674	722	W	J. & W.	Portpatrick	1929-1937
				Relief	1937-1940
1675	723	W	Sir David Richmond of Glasgow	Berwick-on-Tweed	1940-1957
1676	724	W	G.W.	Troon	1929-1955
1694	730	W	Cecil and Lilian Philpott	Moelfre	1930-1956
				Newhaven	1930-1959
				Relief	1959-1969
1695	731	B	Lady Jane and Martha Ryland	Lerwick	1930-1958
				Relief	1958-1969
1696	732	W	Catherine	Bombay	1930-1955

Yard No	Off No	Type	Name	Station(s)	
1575	673	SR	Jane Holland	Selsey	1922-1929
				Eastbourne	1929-1949
				Relief	1949-1953
1576	674	SR	The Newbons	Sennen Cove	1922-1948
				Port St Mary (Isle of Man)	1949-1950
1577	675	SR	V.C.S.	Appledore	1922-1938
				Relief	1938-1945
1573	676	SR	Langham	Bembridge	1922-1939
				Relief	1939-1950
1571	677	W	Prince David	Barry Dock	1922-1937
1568	678	W	Edward, Prince of Wales	Mumbles	1924-1947
1569	679	W	Elizabeth Newton	Hartlepool	1923-1939
				Relief	1939-1953
1570	680	W	City of Bradford (re City of Bradford I)	Humber	1923-1929
				Humber	1929-1932
				Emerg'cy Relief	1932-1952
1572	681	W	K.B.M.	Buckie	1922-1949
				Relief	1949-1952
1586	682	B	William and Kate Johnston	New Brighton	1923-1950
1594	684	W	John R. Webb re 684 RM; re Hearts of Oak	Tenby	1923-1930
				Yarmouth (Isle of Wight)	1934-1938
				Relief	1938-1955
1601	685	W	J. W. Archer	Teesmouth	1924-1950
				Amble	1950-1954
				Relief	1954-1956
1602	686	W	T.B.B.H.	Portrush	1924-1949
				Relief	1949-1953
1610	687	W	B.A.S.P.	Yarmouth	1924-1934
				Falmouth	1934-1940
				Relief	1940-1955
1608	691	N&S	Mary Scott	Valentia	1949-1951
				Southwold	1925-1940
				Relief	1940-1953
1603	694	W	H. F. Bailey re J. B. Proudfoot	Cromer	1924-1928
					1929-1935
1611	695	W	M.O.Y.E.	Porthdinllaen	1925-1949
				Relief	1949-1956
1626	696	B	Robert and Marcella Beck	Plymouth	1926-1938
					1940-1943
					1947-1952

Note: This lifeboat was requisitioned by the Royal Navy and used in Iceland from 1943-1947

Yard No	Off No	Type	Name	Station(s)	
1630	700	W	K.E.C.F.	Rosslare	1927-1939
				Galway Bay	1939-1952
				Relief	1952-1956
1629	701	W	N.T.	Piel/Barrow	1927-1951
				Workington	1952-1953
				Relief	1953-1956

The Troon lifeboat, *Sir David Richmond of Glasgow*, a Watson 40-foot boat built by J. Samuel White's in 1929. *White's Archives*

The Self-Righter *Herbert Joy II* undergoing self-righting tests at East Cowes, prior to entering service at Scarborough in 1931. The tests are being conducted between the Gridiron Yard and what is now the Trinity House Depot. Latterly, White's hammerhead crane was used for self-righting tests on RNLI lifeboats built by all builders at Cowes, including Saunders-Roe and Groves & Guttridge. *David Wilkinson collection*

Yard No	Off No	Type	Name	Station(s)	
1705	736	W	*W. and S.*	Penlee	1931-1960
				Relief	1960-1969
1708	738	SR	*J. H. W.*	Lytham	1931-1938
				Padstow	1939-1947
1709	740	SR	*Cyril and Lilian Bishop*	Hastings	1931-1950
1710	742	SR	*Herbert Joy II*	Scarborough	1931-1951
1711	744	SR	*Laurana Sarab Blunt*	Youghal	1931-1952
1712	746	SR	*William Maynard*	Cloughey	1931-1939
				Relief	1939-1941
				Ferryside	1941-1948
				Whitehills	1948-1949
				Relief	1949-1953
1713	748	SR	*Mary Ann Blunt*	Clogher Head	1931-1950
1718	749	W	*George and Sarah Strachan*	Dunbar	1931-1959
				Relief	1959-1961
				Exmouth	1959-1963
				Relief	1964-1969
1726	751	WB	*Abdy Beauclerk*	Aldeburgh	1931-1959
1731	753	W	*Civil Service No 5*	Donaghadee	1932-1950
				Port St Mary	1950-1956
				Relief	1956-1958
1732	755	B	*Peter and Sarab Blake*	Fenit	1932-1958
				Relief	1958-1972
1734	756	SR	*Civil Service No 4*	Whitehills	1932-1948
1735	757	SR	*Frederick Angus*	Aberystwyth	1932-1949
1745	763	SR	*Caroline Parsons*	St Ives	1933-1938

Yard No	Off No	Type	Name	Station(s)	
1746	764	L	Nellie and Charlie	Anstruther	1933-1950
1747	765	L	Fifi and Charles	Weston-s-Mare	1933-1961
1748	766	L	The Always Ready re Robert Paton re The Always Ready	Runswick	1933-1954
1749	767	SR	Catherine Harriet Eaton	Exmouth	1933-1953
1750	768	SR	Thomas and Annie Wade Richards	Llandudno	1933-1953
1771	771	L	The Three Sisters	Coverack	1934-1954
1772	773	L	Joseph Braithwaite	Maryport Relief	1934-1949 1949-1952
1790	779	S	Rosabella	Ilfracombe	1936-1945
1803	781	L	W. R. A.	North Sunderland Relief	1936-1954 1954-1958
1804	782	L	Margaret Dawson	Gourdon Relief	1936-1952 1952-1955
1810	785	SR	Sir Heath Harrison	Port St Mary Relief	1936-1949 1949-1955
1817	791	L	Elizabeth Wills Allen	Seaham Relief	1936-1950 1950-1953
1818	792	L	Annie, Ronald and Isabella Forrest	St Abbs Scarborough Llandudno	1936-1949 1955-1958 1959-1964
1822	793	L	Clarissa Langdon	Boulmer Relief	1937-1962 1962-1965
1823	794	L	Richard Silver Oliver	Cullercoats Newquay Ilfracombe Criccieth	1937-1939 1940-1945 1945-1953 1953-1961
1831	804	W	S. G. E.	Yarmouth (Isle of Wight) Relief Yarmouth (Isle of Wight)	1938-1943 1943-1945 1945-1963
1832	805	W	Samuel and Marie Parkhouse	Salcombe	1938-1962
1839	814	W	Dunleary II	Dun Laoghaire Lochinver Relief Dunmore East	1938-1967 1967-1968 1968-1972 1972-1973
1840	815	W	Violet Armstrong	Appledore	1938-1962
1871	818	W	Mabel Marion Thompson	Rosslare Harb'r Galway Bay Relief	1939-1952 1952-1968 1968-1974
1872	820	W	Louise Stephens	Gorleston Eyemouth	1939-1967 1967-1974
1873	822	W	Jesse Lumb (orig reg Jessie Lumb)	Bembridge Relief	1939-1970 1970-1980

Yard No	Off No	Type	Name	Station(s)	
5004	828	W	The Princess Royal (Civil Service No 7)	Hartlepool Relief	1939-1968 1968-1976
5005	829	W	Crawford and Constance Conybeare	Falmouth Relief	1940-1968 1968-1970
5006	830	W	Annie Blanche Smith	Dunmore East Relief	1940-1970 1970-1971
5007	835	S	The Gordon Warren	Rhyl Relief	1939-1949 1941-1951
5015	838	W	Michael Stephens	Lowestoft Exmouth Relief	1939-1963 1963-1968 1968-1976
5111	841	W	Manchester and Salford XXIX	Pwllheli Workington Relief	1945-1953 1953-1972 1972-1974
5381	851	SR	Tillie Morrison, Sheffield	Bridlington Llandudno	1947-1953 1953-1959
5398	852	W	Tynesider	Tynemouth Relief	1947-1978 1978-1983
5399	853	W	Winston Churchill (Civil Service No 8)	Blyth Relief	1948-1979 1979-1982
5405	865	W	Elizabeth Rippon	St Helier (Jersey) Relief	1948-1975 1975-1977
5406	866	W	Charles Henry Ashley	Porthdinllaen Relief	1949-1979 1979-1986
5407	867	W	Lady Scott (Civil Service No 4)	Portrush Relief	1949-1981 1982-1986
5416	877	L	George and Caroline Ermen	Clogher Head	1950-1974
5418	883	B	Norman B. Corlett	New Brighton Relief	1950-1973 1973-1981
5419	884	B	St Cybi (Civil Service No 9)	Holyhead Relief	1950-1980 1980-1985
5420	885	W	Sir Samuel Kelly	Donaghadee Relief	1950-1976 1976-1979
5423	887	W	Sir Godfrey Baring	Clacton-on-Sea Wick Workington Relief	1952-1968 1968-1970 1972-1982 1982-1986
5424	888	W	North Foreland (Civil Service No 11)	Margate Relief	1951-1977 1978-1981
5425	889	B	Hilton Briggs	Aberdeen Fenit Relief	1951-1958 1958-1969 1969-1975
5426	890	B	Thomas Forehead and Mary Rouse	Plymouth Relief	1952-1974 1974-1979

Yard No	Off No	Type	Name	Station(s)
5427	898	B	Joseph Hiram Chadwick	Padstow 1952-1967; Galway Bay 1968-1977; Reserve 1977-1979
5428	899	B	City of Glasgow II	Campbeltown 1953-1979
5429	900	W	Herbert Leigh	Barrow 1952-1982; Relief 1982-
5430	901	W	Michael and Lily Davis	Ramsgate 1953-1976; Relief 1976-1979
5431	910	W	Edian Courtauld	Walton-on-Naze 1953-1977; Relief 1977-1981
5432	911	W	City of Bradford III	Humber 1954-1977; Lytham 1978-1985
5433	912	B	Euphrosyne Kendal	St Peter Port 1954-1972; Dunmore East 1973-1975; Relief 1975-1983
5434	913	B	James and Margaret Boyd	Stornoway 1954-1973; Relief 1973-1974; Macduff 1974-1975; Invergordon 1975-1984
5435	923	B	John Gellatly Hyndman	Stronsay 1955-1972; Relief 1972-1984
5436	924	B	Archibald and Alexander M. Paterson	Stromness 1955-1984; Arranmore 1985-1986; Relief 1986-1986; Lowestoft 1986-1987; Relief 1987-
5437	925	W	Henry Comber Brown	Tenby 1955-1986
5438	926	W	Guy and Clare Hunter	St Mary's (Scilly Isles) 1955-1981; Penlee 1982-1983; Relief 1983-1987
5439	929	W	R. A. Colby Cubbin No 1	Douglas (Isle of Man) 1956-1988
5440	930	W	R. A. Colby Cubbin No 2	Port St Mary 1956-1976; Relief 1976-1977
5441	931	W	Richard Vernon and Mary Garforth of Leeds	Angle 1957-1987; Wicklow 1987-1988
5442	932	W	Howard Marryat	Fishguard 1957-1981; Barrow 1982-1986; Moelfre 1986-1988; Workington 1988-1989; Relief 1989-
5466	935	B	R. A. Colby Cubbin No 3	Barra Island 1957-1984
5467	936	B	E. M. M. Gordon Cubbin	Mallaig 1957-1982
5468	940	W	Pentland (Civil Service No 31)	Thurso 1957-1970; Relief 1970-1974; Mumbles 1974-1985; Workington 1986-

Yard No	Off No	Type	Name	Station(s)
5469	945	B	Princess Alexandra of Kent	Torbay 1958-1975; Relief 1975-1983; Tynemouth 1978-1980
5470	946	WB	Alfred and Patience Gottwald	Aldeburgh 1959-1979; Reserve 1979-1980
5495	956	B	John and Frances Macfarlane	Aith (Shetland) 1961-1986
5496	961	O	Calouste Gulbenkian	Weston-s-Mare 1961-1969; Relief 1969-
5520	962	W	T. G. B.	Longhope (Orkney) 1962-1969; Arranmore 1970-1979; Relief 1979-1985
5521	963	W	A. M. T.	Howth 1962-1986; Relief 1986-1989
5522	964	W	The Baltic Exchange	Salcombe 1962-1988
5531	969	W	William Myers and Sarah Jane Myers	Sunderland 1963-1990
5532	970	W	Frederick Edward Crick	Lowestoft 1963-1986
5533	971	W	Joseph Soar (Civil Service No 34)	St Davids 1963-1985; Dunbar 1986-1988; Shoreham 1988-1990
5542	978	O	The Royal Thames	Caister 1964-1969; Runswick 1970-1978; Pwllheli 1979-
5543	979	O	James and Catherine Macfarlane re Amelia	Reserve 1964-1967; Reserve 1967-1978; Scarborough 1978-1991
5544	980	O	William Henry and Mary King	Cromer 1964-1967; Bridlington 1967-1989; Sunderland 1989-1990

The William Henry and Mary King is a 37-foot Oakley type, the last lifeboat built by White's for the RNLI. Based at Cromer in 1964, it was transferred to Bridlington in 1967. *David Wilkinson collection*

APPENDIX 3
VESSELS OWNED BY J. SAMUEL WHITE & CO LTD

Name	Type	Built/acquired
Unnamed	25-foot open launch	1892
Rainham	Coal hulk	1903
Doleful	Fuel lighter	1908
Yard Launch	Motor boat	1912
Cheerily	Fuel lighter	1916
Unnamed	Seaplane tender	1916
Crowpill	Coal barge	1918
Falcon	33-foot motor yard launch	1919
Arreton	98-foot motor barge	1922*
Brighstone	75-foot dumb barge	1922*
Blue Flash	35-foot works service launch	1936
Unnamed	40-foot works service launch	1942
Unnamed	16-foot motor boat	1959

* vessels transferred to Island Transport Co Ltd in 1923

APPENDIX 4
VESSELS OWNED BY ISLAND TRANSPORT CO LTD
(A WHOLLY OWNED SUBSIDIARY COMPANY)

Name	Type	Period
Arreton	98-foot motor barge	1923-74*
Brighstone	75-foot dumb barge	1923-63
Calbourne (I)	Wooden lighter	1924-36
Burlesdon	77-foot steel lighter	1936-56
Debourne	99-foot barge	1936-53
Calbourne (II)	91-foot motor barge	1952-74*
Shalfleet	96-foot motor barge	1962-74*

* vessels sold to the Vectis Shipping Co Ltd in 1974 when Island Transport Co Ltd ceased trading

INDEX